*Advance Praise for*

# CHIVA

This time it takes a village to see the world. Chellis Glendinning
vividly shows through the lens of Chimayó, New Mexico, that local
death can come from global policies. And that the solutions start in
our own hearts and neighborhoods. This book gives us the
heroin questions we will all have to answer.

— Charles Bowden, author of *Down By The River*

*Chiva* is a book of extraordinary complexity and poetical
imagination, a narrative that challenges our assumptions about the
site of healing and the possibilities of belief, without letting us forget
that there is no healing without social justice. A text that both
inspires and radicalizes for social change.

— Marjorie Agosín, professor, Wellesley College, author of
*At the Threshold of Memory* and *Poems for Josefina*

In a sensitve and fluid way, Glendinning reveals the
relationship between economies and cultures in a globalized world
through the commodity heroin, whose consumption has caused so
much pain in her community in New Mexico. Given the failure of
the US's double-standard anti-drug policy, she puts her hopes in a
different strategy: the humanistic approach of harm reduction,
recovery of local cultural traditions, and cohesion of community.

—Luís Astorga, sociologist, Instituto de Investigaciones
Sociales/Universidad Nacional Autónoma de México
(Autonomous University of Mexico)

*Chiva* weaves personal experience and the healing process of
resistance with the effects of drug addiction and colonization in the
context of global economic and political control. A powerful text
that ratifies Chellis Glendinning as one of the most genuine
narrative voices and lucid minds of current American literature.

— Jesús Sepúlveda, author of *The Garden of Peculiarities*

*Chiva* is an excellent book by a gifted and compassionate writer who does a good job as an "outsider" in getting "inside" the life of tecatos and of the culture in general. I like her sophisticated link between rural, sacred place and the global heroin trade.

— Tomás Atencio, sociologist, University of New Mexico

*Chiva*, the book, will be controversial. People locally and nationally will protest, but more will sing its praises as setting a blueprint for hope. I was so taken by the skillful interweaving of four story lines that I laughed and cried, and cursed: the global legitimating of illicit drug profits assisted by political ends and greed; the valiant worldwide fight of land-based peoples against these very ends; the heart wrenching struggle to cleanse the soul of Northern New Mexico from heroin's destructiveness; and the poignant love story between the author and the addict. I read the book in one sitting.

— W. Azul La Luz B., medical sociologist,
University of New Mexico

*Chiva* offers a compelling analysis of the human toll extracted by addiction, while providing a paradigm shift towards treatment based on communal responsibility and the power of the people — all of which can be extrapolated to "Small Town Anywhere, North America."

— Chris Goble, coordinator of a youth withdrawal
management program, Victoria, Canada

Finally, someone has gotten the guts to lay out the bare facts about what heroin is doing to the latinos of northern New Mexico.

— Juan Estevan Arellano, journalist, author of
*Inocencio: Ni pica ni escarda pero siempre de come el mejor elote*

# CHIVA

## A VILLAGE TAKES ON THE GLOBAL HEROIN TRADE

*Chellis Glendinning*

Cataloging in Publication Data:
A catalog record for this publication is available from the National Library of Canada.

Cover design by Diane McIntosh. Image: Fotosearch.
Interior design by Lisa Garbutt. Maps by Bill Sandoval/Buffalo Graphics.

Printed in Canada. First printing January 2005.

Paperback ISBN: 0-86571-513-0

Inquiries regarding requests to reprint all or part of *Chiva: A Village Takes on the Global Heroin Trade* should be addressed to New Society Publishers at the address below.

To order directly from the publisher, please add $4.50 shipping to the price of the first copy, and $1.00 for each additional copy (plus GST in Canada). Send check or money order to:

New Society Publishers
P.O. Box 189, Gabriola Island, BC V0R 1X0, Canada
1-800-567-6772

---

New Society Publishers' mission is to publish books that contribute in fundamental ways to building an ecologically sustainable and just society, and to do so with the least possible impact on the environment, in a manner that models this vision. We are committed to doing this not just through education, but through action. We are acting on our commitment to the world's remaining ancient forests by phasing out our paper supply from ancient forests worldwide. This book is one step towards ending global deforestation and climate change. It is printed on acid-free paper that is 100% old growth forest-free (100% post-consumer recycled), processed chlorine free, and printed with vegetable based, low VOC inks. For further information, or to browse our full list of books and purchase securely, visit our website at: www.newsociety.com

NEW SOCIETY PUBLISHERS
www.newsociety.com

---

**Note to the reader:**
One person in this book is a fictional representation.

The author acknowledges the original publisher of Chapter V, "The Miracle March," *New Age Journal* (January/February 2002).

*Pá los que conocen la tierra*
*y están luchando por ella*

Chimayó is the designated healing place. Its magnetic attraction goes back to the Apaches. It goes back to the beginning of time. Everybody goes there to get healed. But Chimayó is also the village where folks go to buy heroin. This could be tied to the healing: drugs are things people use to try to heal themselves.

*— Ben Tafoya*
*Director of Hoy Recovery Program*
*Española, New Mexico*

# FOREWORD

**By Tom Hayden**

*Chiva* is an elegantly-told struggle with drug addiction that weaves the personal (a lover relapses into heroin) to the community (a small New Mexico village experiences an epidemic) to the global (the war on terrorism revives the poppy trade in Afghanistan) — in a tale that concludes, without preaching, that "healing is one and the same as the work of decolonization."

On any of these levels, the book is interesting enough; but multi-layered, it is stunning. It should be read alongside the works of Luis Rodriguez (*La Vida Loca, Hearts and Hands*) by anyone groping for personal, policy and political alternatives to the failed wars on drugs, gangs and terrorism.

On the most personal level, the most vulnerable, Chellis Glendinning describes a romance that fails between herself, a white woman who moves to the tiny community of Chimayó, New Mexico, and a man named Joaquin Cruz, whose life has consisted of migration, the barrio life of East LA, incarceration, and heroin addiction. His demons apparently are insurmountable, and at one critical moment he admits he's intimidated by her — and too ashamed to accept any help.

Shame is the festering wound of addiction that heroin seems to treat. "The more trivial the cause of the shame, the more intense the feeling of shame," writes Dr. James Gilligan in *Violence*. Shame and addiction visit people of all classes, of course, but shame falls like a blanket on the dispossessed who, by definition, have nothing yet desperately attempt to make a reputation out of that very nothingness. Some of them are literally dying to catch a bullet or kill another as a mirror of themselves. Glendinning describes Joaquin in flight as a "man/child tragically arrested by pain too piercing to remember, clumsily pressing his desperation upon a world as shattered, scattered, and harsh as broken glass."

This is the suicide, she suggests, that arises when the land is taken, the race is humiliated, the language is censured, the culture is rendered feeble, and the weapons of self-destruction are pleasurable. As Franz Fanon wrote of his Algerian patients who experienced a kind of death in life:

[he is] threatened in his affectivity, threatened in his social activity, threatened in his membership in the polis, the North African brings together all the conditions that create a sick man. His first encounter with himself will take place in a neurotic mode... he will feel empty, lifeless, fighting bodily against death, a death that comes before death, death that exists in life.

What to do? Is there a "programmatic" response to addiction, as jobs are a programmatic response to unemployment? Is this where politics and organizing end - in the local cemetery? In Fanon's generation, which lasted from the Algeria of the Fifties to the era of the Black Panthers, the proposed catharsis was personal violence amidst anti-colonial revolution. But experience has shown that such violence, far from withering away in the birth of the "new man," can go on existing in a sort of institutionalized vendetta, or machismo. But one of Fanon's teachings has proven durable, that participation in recovery — on all levels — must be led by the dispossessed themselves. As

Glendinning describes it, the men's and women's groups at the Hoy Recovery Program creating a "fellowship in the spiritual sense"... "creating their own code of ethics for recovery and for life" based on the best of their own traditions.

She doesn't say it, but Glendinning seems to imagine a new revolutionary culture based on recovery groups as a key element in the struggle to replace the system of corporate globalization with its narco-networks, slush funds and unsavory alliances.

Where to begin? Glendinning's answer seems to be that everything must change — and that the macro of everything is reflected in the micro.

She is surprised, given her roots in radical politics, to find herself wanting federal drug agents to bust the local dealers in 1999. She has second thoughts, too, about the merits of drug legalization. "It would transfer the profits to multi-national pharmaceuticals [and] might increase addiction — look at alcohol after prohibition." She draws us into the dilemmas, trade-offs and traps that come with the need for short-term enforcement measures. She might be wrong in her analogy to alcohol prohibition, that addiction to booze rose with its legalization. At least the violence associated with illegal distribution of alcohol declined with the end of

Prohibition, a lesson that is little mentioned in the current debate about drugs. As to legalization increasing addiction, it might be said that the form of alcohol legalization was problematic — the liquor lobby became just that, bankrolling politicians with their profits, plowing unlimited funds into advertising, suppressing studies linking alcohol with violence, minimizing regulation through state alcoholic beverage commissions, and so on. The legalization of drugs could be designed on a medical model rather than a corporate one, but Glendinning's caution about drug legalization is reality-based and brave.

Most important is her description of community-based efforts to deal with addiction outside the criminal justice system. Her stories of the Hoy Recovery Program and a mobilization by indigenous people invoke the idea of community healing among a people whose land, traditions and economic livelihood have been stolen by outsiders. In her hopeful view, the communal life of Chimayó in its entirety must became a self-managed rehabilitation program. La cultura cura.

Chellis Glendinning once again is to be thanked for sharing her maps of the personal, the bioregional, cultural and global. One can only wish that the elites of corporate globalization would read her story and respond. Instead they seem bent on displacing blame for the "coming anarchy" on the dispossessed underclass itself. Robert Kaplan, for example, stimulates First World fears with his claims that globalization is "Darwinian":

It means economic survival of the fittest — those groups and individuals that are disciplined, dynamic and ingenious will float to the top, while cultures that do not compete well technologically will produce an inordinate number of warriors [animated by] the thrill of violence...slaughter and blood and the choking groans of men.

Against these apocalyptic predictions, Glendinning's focus on one small crossroads of the world may seem hopeless. But there is a sense of hope throughout this painful book, based on the faith that those who have survived thus far in the crevices of capitalism and colonialism are yet able to recover their capacities to live as free human beings.

TOM HAYDEN

December 2004

[Tom Hayden has been involved in progressive social movements for four decades. He served 18 years in the California legislature and has written 10 books, including *Street Wars: Gangs and the Future of Violence*.]

# CHIVA

# I.

**D**ragon made His first appearance in *el norte* as an ink stamp on the wooden cartons that came up from the hills of Sinaloa. He showed up again after World War II, traveling on burlap sacks from Mexico, maybe Turkey. Then He came stuffed into duffle bags from Southeast Asia. He seems to like northern New Mexico, this beast, for He has made the journey again and again — even from such far-away places as Burma, Afghanistan, and Colombia.

He's here now, in fact, strutting through the halls of Española Valley High School, riding the backs of polyester shirts.

# II.

*El norte.*

Here the blood of the people braids intertwining rivulets of Toltec, Mayan, Spanish, Moor, Apache, Tewa, Dine', Lebanese, and Greek. Here the language is a mountain mix of Castilian Spanish, Mexican native, and local indigenous — overlaid now with phrases garnered from corporate TV talk and fragments of African-American street language that can be traced to the invasion of the boom box.

As an expatriate from what's locally dubbed "the dominant society," I fit right into this northern New Mexico Chicano world. Or at least I do now that I have navigated the inevitable hurdles and hoops thrust in my face during my first decade of inhabiting the adobe house "behind Montoya's hardware, over the river, under the wooden cross." Not the least of these hurdles has been the drug world — the trafficking, shooting up, syringes along the riverbank, burglaries, throat-slittings, police presence, and prison culture associated with the abuse of *chiva*, or heroin. I almost wrote "drug underworld," but in fact there is no underworld here. One of the truths of a culture with roots in land and ancestry is that no facet of the community is separate from, or unknown to, any other facet. Even the stated philosophy that blows across the buffalo grass of this blessed *mal país* rejects the dualities of experience and thought proffered by the dominant society, relishing instead to celebrate the strange beauty of life's ever-meshing energies and phenomena. Indeed, I count as my friends chile farmers as well as bank robbers, drug dealers along with state troopers, community organizers and ex-cons. I have learned to open my heart to a wisdom that does not flee from suffering, breakdown, or error; rather the wisdom of this place knows these aspects of life as inseparable from joy, triumph, and communion.

We need such wisdom. In 2002 the United Nations conservatively estimated that international trafficking of illicit drugs takes up 8 percent of world trade — in the ballpark of $500 to $700 billion a year — more than iron, steel, and motor vehicles; more than textiles, tourism, or legal pharmaceuticals.[1] Abuse of all drugs is on the rise, and heroin especially. Worldwide production doubled between the mid-1980s and the mid-1990s, rose by 20 percent in 1996, and may have increased by another 25 percent by 2002.[2] The United States Drug Enforcement Administration reports that by 2002 the number of addicts in the US had grown to 977,000 — with another 514,000 using heroin occasionally.[3] According to historian Alfred McCoy, 0.7 percent of Americans, or 1.96 million, are addicts,[4] while the US Public Health Service estimates that 3.1 million Americans — one in every 100 — have consumed the drug at some point in their lives.[5]

Against this backdrop, the release of a New Mexico Department of Health report was expected to unravel us. Quite frankly it did not, for in our guts we already knew: between 1993 and 1995 our state was #1 in per-capita deaths from illicit drug overdoses. The county I live in, Río Arriba, weighed in at #1 in the state, leading all other counties by more than five to one. And it was already over-the-back-fence knowledge that the village of Chimayó where I live harbored the most dealers and users, or *tecatos*, in the county. In other words, right here *we were #1*. The report also noted that Río Arriba ranked second in DWI deaths — while murder, often associated with substance abuse, occurred at three times the state average.[6]

Indeed, at the time of the report, things were dire. I will begin by telling you that Río Arriba is "Third World" rural. According to the 2000 US Census, only 34,000 people inhabit a county the size of the state of Massachusetts; 73 percent are Spanish- or Mexican-American, 14 percent have Native American roots, and 12 percent are European American, while three-quarters of the people speak Spanish or native tongues like Tewa, Diné, or Apache. The county is also "Third World" poor. During the 1990s the average household income was $14,263 —in many villages per-capita income was under $5000 — and each year at the time the snow dusted the valley between the Sangre de

Cristo and Jemez mountains, unemployment swelled to 20 percent.[7]

Río Arriba is a happy place in the sense that simplicity and gratefulness infuse the people's hearts; nothing compares to hanging out at Orlando's general store and chewing the fat about the latest twist on the clouds' ability to deliver rain. But Río Arriba is not a happy place in the sense that simplicity and gratefulness do not lend themselves to the demands of the growing onslaught of dominant society technologies, wage-earner time schedules, New York prices — and that six-lane monstrosity barreling its way north toward our pasture lands.

Yes, when the Department of Health report came out, things were dire. Hypodermic needles, soda-can cookers, and broken Bud bottles littered the village, and everywhere *vatos*, or homeboys, could be seen staggering like wounded dragons down Route 76. Everywhere *tecatos* shot off their 30.06s, broke into people's homes, and rampaged over the dirt roads in low-slung sedans with black-tinted windows. The summer of 1998 we endured two murders in the space of one week: Danny Chavez's body was discovered in an apple orchard, shot in the head; Anthony

Martinez was killed by a bullet shot through the roof of his mouth. The *tecatos* ruled. And they promised to continue their reign by offering each generation coming up through middle school the full array of addictive possibilities.

Is the iron gate open or closed? It's open. You look left, then right. You check the parking lot at Montoya's hardware for cop cars. If nothing's in the way, you pull in. Drive over the gravel to the pump house. With his boxer shorts protruding over the waistband of his jeans, Brian Gallegos is stretching at the door jam to the nearby shed. He ambles over to your car. *"Chiva,"* you say and hand him a ten and a five. He leans his elbow on your open window and glances up toward the cottonwood tree as if he's having a casual chat. Then he opens his hand and a pellet the size of a BB drops into yours. You back up. You gun it across Route 76, down the dirt road to the bridge.

I am walking to the Santuario today to pray. From my house the mile-and-a-half journey across the badlands passes by the pink turrets of sand we call *barrancas*, twists through labyrinthine *arroyos*, and jumps several *acequias*, or irrigation ditches, before arriving at the church.

Talk about contrasts. It is almost Lent now, mid-February. Soon the people walking to El Santuario will not be villagers like myself or the everyday pilgrims that arrive in a low-key stream throughout the year. No, come Good Friday, 30,000 people will land in our village of 3,000 like a buffalo in the gullet of a garden snake. Chimayó may be the home of the greatest number of drug dealers in the county with the most overdose deaths in the US; it is also the spiritual center of the Río Grande Valley.

For centuries pilgrims have been trudging across the mountain desert to the clearing beneath Chimayó's juniper-speckled hills. First the native people came, usually on foot, some from pueblos as far away as a hundred miles. The springs were bubbling up by the river then, and the travelers drank the water. They also made balls of the mud they believed would catalyze healing, and they carried these home to their ailing relatives. In time the springs dried up, and the Spanish arrived. To pad their efforts at settlement, the Spanish brought with them native people from Mexico — Chimayó's original grant of land was named with them in mind, La Merced de Santa Cruz de la Cañada de los Mexicanos — and they too identified the place as a nexus of healing and its now-arid soil as miraculous. In 1813 the settlers built the Santuario out of the sacred earth and textured the faith practiced here with rites and *santos* from the south.

Nuestra Señora de Guadalupe made Her way to this outpost of miracles. She Who Comes Flying from the Region of Light like an Eagle of Fire. Tlecuauhtlacupeuh. Faith through no-matter-what distresses befall the people.

The dark-skinned El Señor de Esquípulas emerged, literally from the soil, to hang with His arms outstretched above the altar. Compassion.

El Santo Niño de Atocha, clad in a cape the color of the sky. He trudges through the *mal país* at night, helper to wounded travelers and lost souls.

I arrive at the Santuario with dried-out thorns festooning my socks. My goal is to sit in prayer in the nave and then to enter the *posito* for a handful of Holy

Dirt. I pause outside. Silence hangs like humidity. No *tecatos* are in sight, but the factory-made signs ringing the parking lot — PLEASE LOCK VALUABLES IN YOUR VEHICLE — are reminders that stand in contrast to the hand-clasping, eye-lowering humility of today's pilgrims. I slip into the cool of the sanctuary. Soon there will be snow-cone vendors galore, TV-news helicopters clipping the air overhead, and an impromptu parade of Chimayó's finest low-rider cars.

Good Friday is just six weeks away.

I met the ex-con and former drug dealer I almost married at the Chamisa Lounge in the nearby town of Española, also right before the launch of Lent. The Spanish word *casi* is useful here. Normally it means "almost" — as in *casi nunca* or "almost never." Paradoxically, when *casi* is combined with *indio*, the resulting *casindio* does not translate to "almost Indian." It means "always Indian" and refers to the urge many Chicanos feel to dismantle the monolith of Hispanic identity thrust upon them and reclaim their native roots. I like to think I am *casi casada* —

almost married into the culture by my near-liaison with Señor Joaquin Cruz and at the same time always married into it by my unceasing and, at times, cursed love for it.

Joaquin let me in on his past with considerable caution. Perhaps he harbored fear that I might not take to it with the same eagerness the Russian olive, upon its arrival, took to the Española valley. I knew Joaquin for three years before he spilled the *frijoles*.We were sitting on the couch in his old family home in Chimayó. That house! It seemed to me that someone had taken a machine gun to the walls. The plastering was mottled with holes that looked like prehistoric cave paintings of bison hoofprints, and someone had methodically stabbed the floor with a pick axe. There was no electricity, no heat, no telephone. Out back the weathered carcass of a toilet squatted next to the same *acequia* that had been excavated by the first sixteen families pioneering the settlement in the 1700s.

Joaquin and I were talking about the ancient prophesies of the Hopi people, wildly gesticulating with our hands as we amassed evidence for the prediction that around about this moment in history we humans would be going to self-made hell.

"And ... and ... the Hopi said a gourd filled with ashes would fall from the clouds. That's the atom bomb!" I gasped. "They said there would be a big house in the sky. The space station! And children would be killing children. It's all happening!"

"Aaaaaiiii! How you say it is how it is!" he blurted out. "It is so bad the elk they are all sick in the *monte!* It is so bad the children they are afraid to go to school. It is so bad ..."he shrieked,"... you cannot even rob a bank no more!"

I stopped. Ah ... what? Did ... *you* ... rob banks?

Well. Yes.

What he meant was that the code of honor he had followed as a criminal had gone to hell. Things were in such a sad state that it had become dangerous to continue in the profession. Joaquin had robbed banks around East Los Angeles in the 1960s and '70s as a way, he said, to sabotage institutions like Bank of America and Safeway that were stealing from his people. The new crop of robbers had no purpose, he insisted; they robbed just to get high from the intensity of the experience. Worse, they did not take care of each other.

In preparation for the coming pilgrimage, county crews are cleaning up the most worn roadways into Chimayó. I see them carting their bulging plastic bags up Juan Medina Road. Several are from Chimayó, the others from Española and the neighboring village of Córdova. "Wayne, ¿como estás? Got any new lambs this spring?" "Sí. Pero not yet. Te llamaré." When the men are finished, the road will appear as pristine as it was when those sixteen families navigated it with all their earthly possessions crammed onto burro-drawn wagons.

More than earthly possessions litters this highway now. By today's standards, you could say that much of it is typical roadside trash: disposable diapers, old newspapers, broken television sets, pop bottles, tennis shoes. But then there's something else. An aluminum soda can sliced in two to make a heroin cooker. A rubber tourniquet. A slew of used syringes. In just six weeks thousands of pilgrims will walk along this road singing and reciting the rosary. The sky will be big and turquoise, the roadway lined with the pastel-green shoots of chamisa and sage. Likely, the pilgrims will not think about the activities that preceded them.

I am thinking about them. They are part of life in Chimayó. Before the drug bust of 1999, my house was sandwiched between the village's two biggest merchants, the Barelas and the Gallegoses. I had met Bobby Barela years before when he came selling firewood to my rented mobile home north of Santa Fe. After he stacked the wood, I looked into his black eyes and thanked him. "You've helped me a lot," I said, happy that come fall I would not go cold. He answered with a smirk. "You've helped me more," and two days later the house was broken into: TV, VCR, and family jewelry all stolen, and the entire bedroom, including books and clothes, picked over and strewn across the carpet. I met up with Bobby again when I moved next door to the Barela compound in Chimayó. I hardly got to see him though. Two months later he was dead on the floor of his trailer from a heroin overdose.

Brian Gallegos was a different story. He sidled up to my table at the Chamisa Lounge to introduce himself. He had pimples. He also had a rudely-executed tattoo on his inside left arm proclaiming, in Old English typeface, his son's name: STEPHEN. My first inkling that Brian was on heroin came on the dance floor. Everyone else was prancing and gyrating across the linoleum; Brian moved in lumbering slow motion.

I developed a strategy for surviving in the midst of the drug reign. If there were, as state police estimated, 150 users in Chimayó,[8] and if each committed one crime a week to support his habit, then 600 villagers would be hit up each month. Or 300, each twice. It was your basic when-not-if situation. Clearly, any survival strategy I might devise would have to involve extraordinary means.

To begin, I spent six hours walking the periphery of my yard drumming and burning sage. Then I sought out what we might call "lite" acquaintance with the dealers, arms length but respectful — and explicit in its meaning: "I'm here. You're here. I won't get in your way." My immediate neighbor, an Anglo newcomer like myself, remained aloof. In fact, she avoided contact with everyone and spoke of the villagers like a racist. (She was a real estate developer.) Her house was robbed on a regular basis. Mine was never robbed.

Joaquin was not "lite" acquaintance. He had skin the color of deer, lines etched into his face like petroglyphs, and an irrepressible twinkle. He also had the body of a man with time enough to pump iron. Most of all, he listened. He was without artifice and deeply kind.

We were friends and, because we both loved the *norteño* music reverberating through this upland desert, occasional dance partners. I'm sure we cut an odd portrait on the dance floor. Me: Anglo with heritage in Wales, Scotland, England, and Holland; him: Chicano with roots in the Yaqui and White Mountain Apache tribes. Me: five-foot-seven (five-nine in cowboy boots); him: five-foot-three in his East LA flat shoes. Me with a PhD; him with a rap sheet the length of my curriculum vitae.

What brought us together was soul. Believe me, I fought it. Disregarded it. Denied it. Looked elsewhere. But in the end, I had to acknowledge the power that infused us.

The moment of not-turning-back occurred in the summer of 2000. Joaquin was a court-ordered participant in Drug Court. Rather than returning him to Los Lunas Medium Security Prison after a parole violation stemming from an altercation with his parole officer, the judge gave Joaquin an opportunity: to participate in Amistad, the first outpatient heroin-recovery program in the Española valley. Although Joaquin had broken from heroin addiction six years earlier, Drug Court was a chance to be supported in putting his life back together.

One of the other Amistad participants was giving a party on a Sunday afternoon. Clients, counselors, and administrators were playing horseshoes and barbecuing homegrown lamb in the plaza of the village of Alcalde. The hostess asked Joaquin to pick flowers for the table, and we set out across the chile fields like children of sunshine. We arrived at *la presa*, the place where the *acequia* diverts water to the village from the Río Grande. The water was rushing by with crushing force. Ravens dove and glided overhead. I was overcome with a presence so powerful my fingers quivered. The river. The sun. The birds. The pebbles. The trout. His hands. Our hearts.

Everything we did together felt like a celebration — from the seeming burden of attending court hearings to cooling our late-summer bodies between the rocks of the Santa Cruz river. We cooked salmon on an open fire. We shopped for deals in Santa Fe's thrift stores. We got a puppy. We were in love, and by outside accounts our love radiated an aura the size of the county.

My initiation into the full weight of Joaquin's past unfolded slowly. Because I gave him compassion rather than judgment, he edged toward a sense of freedom about himself.

He had grown up in Chimayó. His father had been a chile farmer, an elk hunter, and a participant in the sacred brotherhood known as Los Hermanos Penitentes; his mother a gardener and caretaker to her six children. The cash economy arrived in full force only after World War II, and as its requirements and inequities supplanted traditional land-based livelihoods, a desperate poverty emerged. Food became scarce. No one seemed to have anything, and fear was epidemic. Meanwhile, tales of good industrial jobs in southern California blew through the villages like a March gale.

The family drove a borrowed '47 Chevy to Los Angeles. Renting a tenement in the African-American section known as Watts, both Cruz parents left the rootedness of their Río Arriba lives to be factory workers, and the events that lay the foundation for Joaquin's future difficulties began.

It's hard to know exactly what these events were. When bad things happen, the mind has a way of shredding like confetti into a parade of amnesia. Then there's the family. The secrets of the family can be locked in place like the metal doors of a prison cell. Just the simple act of reminiscing becomes an insurmountable hurdle. Nobody knows for sure. But one thing we do know: *something* happened.

Maybe it started with Señor Cruz. Maybe the demands and contradictions of being a man with a family to support, no money in his pocket — and the smell of ponderosa needles within memory — pushed him over the edge. Maybe he initiated a no-room-for-error regime of discipline, and maybe when his country brood inevitably failed to live up to his rules, he stood them in a tight line and, with a leather cow strap, walloped them until they bled. Maybe, when Señora Cruz tried to intercede he turned on her, raging like a bear — and the children saw it all. Or perhaps he jumped into the Chevy and rammed its chrome bumper into the cinder block railing behind the building. Then one day in the midst of this newly-instituted urban terror, maybe another violence arose. Maybe a gang of black boys, all older and bigger, chased Joaquin into the alley. Maybe they threw him against the California sand and took turns punching him. Maybe he ran crying to his father, and instead of offering solace the elder Cruz exploded, ordering his son to track down each of his attackers and beat him up. Maybe just maybe, out of terror and even more out of a need to gain his father's approval, Joaquin obeyed.

At a certain point and maybe it was just after these things happened, the Cruzes moved to an apartment on Pleasant Street in the Boyle Heights *barrio* of East LA. This period launched Joaquin into even more confusion about authority and love. His father, now making a little more money, enrolled the children in parochial school. He bought them uniforms to wear, a suit and tie for Joaquin and jumpers for the girls. Most notably, Mr. Cruz gave Joaquin a dazzling prize: a fine silver-flecked shirt in the '50s boxy style that was so popular. But maybe, at the same time, he also continued to whip his son.

Beyond all that, maybe there was something even more that compounded Joaquin's inner struggle. Maybe, in a desperate search for goodness and safety, even beauty, Joaquin turned to his mother's chosen sanctuary, the Catholic Church. He did become an altar boy, this we know. But maybe the priest-father he now looked to for acceptance turned on him, and, red robes lifted over his face, maybe the whole world became hell.

And if these things happened, the year would have been 1957. Joaquin would have been eight years old.

It is said that the drug bust of 1999 changed Chimayó forever. The statement is true. But there are still dealers, and there are still users. A car full of them has been stopping by the bridge to shoot up. I guess I've become inured because, to my mind, they can shoot up here as well as anywhere else. The thing that gets my goat is that these *tecatos* are class-A litterbugs. They are throwing their syringes out the car window, naked and uncapped, and the perhaps disease-contaminated needles are lying there in the dirt like angry sticker thorns.

I stop by the metal barrack that is the Española station of the New Mexico State Police. Officer Mark Lewandowski is earnest about his work. His breathing quickens as he tells me about the danger he faces patting down *tecatos* who harbor syringes in their pockets.

He describes a Chimayoso on drugs who, sustaining a minor injury to his nose, was so crazed he chopped it off with a butcher knife. I try to give as much detail as I can about the car on the bridge: early '80s sedan, four-door, weather-worn black with tinted windows. At this point Officer Lewandowski stands up. In his crisp black uniform he is a full six feet tall. From up there near the fluorescent fixtures, he rails against the state-run needle exchange program.

I am surprised. Its purpose is to prevent the transmission of disease by supplying clean syringes. Any thinking person would be in favor of such an effort, and indeed every institution that has studied it — the National Academy of Sciences, the American Public Health Association, the World Health Organization, the United Nations Programme on HIV/AIDS — agrees that access to sterile needles is a good thing. US cities offering needle exchange have an 11 percent lower rate of increase in HIV.[9] One program in Connecticut has documented a 33 percent reduction.[10]

Through some stroke of public health fate, the problem in New Mexico is not so much HIV; it is hepatitis. Eighty-two percent of drug users here suffer from the highly contagious hepatitis C, 61 percent from hepatitis B.[11] According to Lewandowski — and his conviction reveals the truth that nothing in the drug world is simple — the now-familiar RV that hands out drug paraphernalia each Tuesday morning is having an adverse effect in the community: the number of syringes people are turning in adds up to less than the number handed out, and users are discarding them about the village like candy wrappers.

Lewandowski pledges to track down the black sedan and get the bridge cleaned up. He also wonders aloud who in the neighborhood might be dealing. *Tecatos* are people with zero patience. When they buy drugs, they don't usually make it more than a quarter mile from the dealer's driveway before they shoot up.

# III.

Joaquin howled when I told him I was thinking about writing a book about *chiva*. I said I wanted to write an essay on heroin, and he just doubled over. You see, in English the word "essay" sounds like the Spanish *ese*, and an *ese* on heroin translates to: a cold-stoned, street-smart homeboy.

*Norteños* say that the Española valley has harbored *eses* on heroin for some time — at least since the 1950s. Each village might have had one or two users back then, they say, and then consumption became widespread in the 1970s after the Vietnam War. Others point to the late 1980s as the time when heroin addiction, along with the crime and disease that accompany it, became endemic.

1957: East LA. Joaquin climbs onto the roof of his family's apartment in Boyle Heights. From his perch he can see right into the window of the apartment next door. There is a man standing in the bathroom, a man Joaquin has seen around the neighborhood. The *ese* lowers his window shade, and against the glaring illumination of a bare light bulb, his silhouette filters through the screen like a Rorschach blot. Joaquin watches. Oddly, the man swings his arm in circles. Around and around and around. Then he pumps up his muscles and pokes something — Joaquin cannot make out what — into the inner bend of his arm. The man then turns out the light and moments later reappears in the backyard. He digs a hole and buries a package in it.

Silently, stealthily, with the curiosity of a city cat, Joaquin drops himself into the yard and, with his fingers, scoops out the dirt. He discovers a rubber balloon. Something is hidden inside. When Joaquin disentangles the knot, a pungent vinegary cloud envelops him.

No. 3 heroin/Brown Sugar. Charcoal gray and lumpy. 40 percent pure. No. 3 is made by mixing morphine with hydrochloric acid and activated charcoal. Stir in flavorings like caffeine, quinine, or strychnine. Ready? Place a crumb on a piece of aluminum foil. Light from below with a match. Chase the Dragon: suck in the fumes with a rolled-up piece of paper. Play the Mouth Organ: use a matchbook cover.

No. 3/White Dragon Pearl. This is better. It's chalky white, 50 percent pure, and cut with barbituate barbitone. Grind it into a grainy powder. Unfurl a cigarette and sprinkle it into the tobacco. Rewrap the cigarette. Shoot the Ack-Ack Gun: smoke in staccato puffs.

Odds are that the heroin injected by Joaquin's neighbor in East LA, as well as the heroin making its way into northern New Mexico, arrived via the Turkey-Marseilles route known as the French Connection. Right after World War II, the US government pressured Italy and other countries making pharmaceutical morphine to tighten regulations so that none would spill over into the illegal trade. The time was ripe to eliminate all heroin consumption. The war had disrupted shipping routes from France and the Middle East, and Mao Tse-Tung's campaign to ban opium production and clean up China's addiction had put a halt to imports from Asia. Inside the US, a dwindling 20,000 addicts were left to poke about the streets for what could hardly be found.[12]

And yet an inconsistency was brewing within the US government that, through time, would become standard. Due to contradictions of perception caused by post-war exigencies, Washington began to proclaim "Just Say No" with its right hand — while with its left, it was launching the covert alliances with world-class drug traffickers that have characterized American policy ever since and, in their stead, have increased global narcotics production.

The first such alliance was with a rough bunch, a syndicate of Corsican gangsters congregated in Marseilles. The Corsicans saw the US as a market waiting to flourish — it had been the world's second largest in the 1930s — and their goal was to glut the country with the forbidden elixir. They succeeded. By 1952 the population of addicts mushroomed from its postwar low of 20,000 to 60,000; by 1965 it had reached 150,000.[13]

The production cycle began in Turkey. Watch this. It's archetypal. You will see it repeated throughout the history of the illicit narcotics trade.

Turkish honchos in cahoots with Corsican gangsters coerced peasant farmers to grow opium. *(In poor countries, farmers who have traditionally grown food for their own communities are forced — by economics, at gunpoint, or both — to grow narcotics.)* The traffickers then commandeered the peasants to refine the sap into bricks of morphine, which they passed to hired smugglers. The smugglers slipped these from Turkey, through Lebanon, to Marseilles. *(Couriers carry the drug in transportable form.)* Once in Marseilles, in downtown tenements and villas scattered across the countryside, chemists transformed the morphine into the kind of

high-grade heroin American users had come to crave:
no. 4. *(The morphine is turned into the preferred product.)*
Next, via a slippery labyrinth of routes through
Canada and the Caribbean, they brought the drug to
New York City. *(It is transported to the country of use.)*
Waiting Sicilian-American distributors — read: Mafia
— trucked it to dealers in cities across the eastern
seaboard of the United States. *(It is sold.)*

Through the years the US government participated
in this web in tangled ways — sometimes by complici-
ty, other times by turning a blind eye, still others by
actively funding, transporting, dealing, and making
use of the profits — always impelled by the paranoias,
projections, and exigencies of the Cold War.

The motivation? The port of Marseilles was not
just home to Corsican drug dealers. It was the strong-
hold of the French Communist Party. The dock workers there had endured unspeakable conditions for
years, often working long, sweaty hours without making enough money to eat. They had fought for a living
wage since the 1930s. They had organized against dis-
proportionate taxes that further depleted their
incomes, against their country's military involvement
in Indochina — and against drug smuggling. On the

other side, the narcotics-dealing Corsicans formed an anti-communist underground. In the 1930s they had fought alongside French Fascists to stamp out worker-rights demonstrations and during the war had allied themselves with the Nazi Gestapo. They were the perfect group to aid the US in its postwar campaign to squelch communism — full of dockside muscle and dedicated to whoever would help them do business.

The workers went on strike in 1947, holding spirited mass meetings and marching through the streets. At their pinnacle the red flag waved over the Palace of Justice. They appeared to be taking control of the city, and the French government wasn't stopping them. Alarmed at the possibility of losing France to communism, the US secretly dispatched six agents of its newly formed Central Intelligence Agency — three veterans of wartime intelligence and three "representatives" of the American labor movement[14] — who, upon arrival, stuffed the Corsicans' bank accounts with US taxpayer dollars.

So began the battle between the Mob and the Reds. With covert backing from the US, the Corsicans had the resources to fight with abandon — to harass union officials, assault picket lines, beat up city officials, murder strikers, threaten witnesses, and fill in as scabs. They triumphed, and with their newly won mastery over docks, local government, foreign relations, even over their Mafia rivals in Italy and the US, the Corsicans landed the formidable position of the world's top traffickers — by 1965 supplying 80 percent of what, because of the surge in availability, became an expanding US market.[15]

And the CIA slithered on to its next skirmish with communism.

Slither on. It's also possible that the *chiva* Joaquin glimpsed in 1957 got into East LA from Mexico. Not because of any monopoly Mexico had over the market or because of any greasing of the biz by the US — but, plain and simple, because of Mexico's closeness to the American Southwest.

Heads up on this one. If you hail from the dominant society, you may have to make a conceptual leap: in a community that makes its livelihood directly from the land — even when that community is uprooted, when Chevys come to replace horses and dollar bills take over for apples and mutton — knowledge is not transmitted so much by newspaper source or research document. It moves by word of mouth.

Books purport to lay down the facts; heroin first made its way across *la frontera* after World War II, they claim. But at Orlando Martinez's general store in Chimayó, it is said that opium was cultivated in the Mexican state of Sinaloa long before, a labor of entrepreneurial Chinese workers who immigrated in the 1880s when President Porfirio Díaz was attempting to expand his country's international clout by trading with China. The Sierra Madre highlands just inland from the coast were perfect for growing: warm, wet, and remote. Remembering that opium had built an empire for the British, the Chinese were eager to carve out a profitable niche in their adopted country, and the *camino reales* winding north were already well trod from centuries of indigenous exchange and more recent conquistadoring by the Spanish.

Opium found its way along these corridors.

Opium. The sticky brown sap lanced from the head of the poppy plant. 3-17 percent morphine. Place a dab in a smoking pipe. Light with a stick of incense. Inhale. Or try this: mix with wine, saffron, and cinnamon in a tincture bottle. Squeeze four droplets into water. Sip.

Hang around Orlando's. It is said too that opium was the favored high among *viejos* in America's *barrios* in 1957. The newer, injectable stuff was used by returning servicemen, and what with a postwar abundance of money and jobs, many — maybe that *ese* next door — could maintain their habits while living ordinary lives. Curiously, despite a 1940s scheme by New York gangster Harold Meltzer to make Mexico a major supplier, the amounts shipped north were minor. They entered largely through border towns like Nogales and Tijuana, and the opiate trade — begun by the Chinese, picked up by Mexican dealers, and *(as with most profit-hungry endeavors in poor countries)* intertwined with the state system perpetrated by the Party of Institutionalized Revolution — proceeded on its own through local connections and local effort.

1972: Joaquin is twenty-three, not-free, and not-white. The formal education his father has pressed upon him has turned into a roller-coaster ride of peaks and screaming descents. He has distinguished himself in school as *una guítarrista fina* and been mentored to study both *la vihuela*, or Spanish lute, and the traditional guitar known as *el requinto*. He has also been booted out of a slew of schools for his angry outbursts at authority in the persons of Catholic priests. All around him are gangs and guns. And drugs. When he walks through the playground to school, there are drugs. When he goes to parties in the *barrio*, there are drugs. When he hangs out in the alley, there are drugs. He is quick to fathom the possibilities: some boys follow their frustrated fathers into factory work; others drive dazzlingly low-slung Cadillacs, claim their manhood with tattoos and sharkskin suits, and deal in danger.

Joaquin bats between the two worlds, the *mestizo* and the *pachuco*, the upstanding and the criminal. He does indeed study the musical influences that make up *el estilo Chicano*, is recognized as a young man with professional places to go, and is hired to play in *orquestas* and *bandas*.

He also shoots up.

That first time is like a gateway to paradise. He copies what the others do. Nervously he belts his left bicep with a bandana and pumps up the muscles until the veins bulge. Then, with his right hand, he stabs the needle into the vein in the bend of his left arm. His fingers shake as he backs the syringe up, sucking a few drops of his own blood out, then quickly presses the pusher so the liquid surges in. Thirty seconds after he slides the needle out, there it is: a feeling of peace as he has never known it. Warmth. Happiness. It starts in his belly and radiates outward like a star. Euphoria. Communion.

It's hard to tell which Joaquin became addicted to first: robbing banks or shooting up. Robbing banks seemed an unusually potent way to say "Fuck You" to his father. It was also a way to acquire what society deemed valuable, money, when what was truly valuable — his parents' care and protection — had proven elusive. The narcotic high could have been a way to blot out the conflict he harbored between love and terror, need and anger. It could also have been a way of putting his suffering on display. Or calling for help.

Joaquin took to his chosen activities with the persistence of a person driven by overlapping motivations.

By 1972 he was working for a drug lord running heroin from Mexico to LA. On his own, he was robbing his politically-chosen targets.

One thing we know about the business: it's persistent. When squelched by police work, prohibition, or political upheaval in one location, it migrates to another. Quickly. Deliberately. Almost as if someone were orchestrating its movement.

The heroin Joaquin injected in 1972 did not come from Turkey. In the late 1960s and early '70s, a series of events took place that signaled what appears to be an intentional reshaping of the narcotics business.

In 1968 the US Mafia's top importer, Santo Trafficante Jr., made a foray to tap new supply networks in Hong Kong, Singapore, and Saigon. The trip was odd. Trafficante had access to all the No. 4 he could ever need from the Corsicans in Marseilles.

Then, out of the blue, the US contributed $35 million to Turkey to stamp out their entire opium crop.[16] In 1970 President Nixon went all out for rapprochement with the French government, from which the US had been estranged since the hot and heavy days of Marseilles. The ostensible purpose of the reunion was to join together to fight the scourge of drugs — with an emphasis on crushing the Corsicans who since the '40s ...(heads up) ... *had commandeered more business than the US Mafia.* Meanwhile, Nixon set up his infamous espionage outfit, the Special Investigation Unit, otherwise known from Watergate as the Plumbers. Its purpose was to rout out all opposition to US policy. But the Plumbers didn't just track anti-communist activities; several of its members actually doubled as associates of Trafficante and spent their time collecting intelligence on drug operations in competition with Trafficante.[17]

It could appear that the US government and the Mafia were in cahoots. And it seems it had happened before — what with the CIA, JFK, and a gang of Mafioso hitmen coalescing to off Fidel Castro at the Bay of Pigs in 1961. And, in a parallel universe, the Feds were throwing grand juries to jail syndicate leaders. The left hand and the right. The shrouded and the upstanding. The power-mongering and the expedient.

1972: moralistic grandstanding was ringing from the rafters in DC. "If we cannot destroy the drug menace in America," declared Nixon, "it will destroy us!"[18]

— all the while supplies of heroin coming into the country were increasing. The number of addicts tripled from 250,000 in 1969 to 750,000 by 1972.[19]

But the heroin wasn't coming from Turkey and Marseilles. No. Joaquin's first fix more likely came from the source Trafficante and his brood had been eyeing: the Golden Triangle of Southeast Asia.

The Golden Triangle is an area that extends from the hills of northeastern Burma through the mountain ridges of Thailand to the highlands of north Laos. Coincident with the fall of the Turkey-Marseilles connection, the opium business in Southeast Asia began to stretch beyond self-sufficiency to become a full-blown source for international export.

Burma-Thailand-Bangkok. Here's a story strikingly similar to the one you just heard. *Communist success engenders capitalist freak-out. Local farmers are wrenched from self-sufficiency into commodity production. The US, or its allies, lure native tribes into the military project in exchange for help with their cash crop. As the effort to squelch communism grows, the opium crop grows. As the crop grows, distribution mushrooms. With more distribution, more people become addicts.*

After World War II, Chiang Kai-chek's capitalist-leaning Nationalist China collapsed, and Mao's Communist China took power. In an attempt to stem the southerly flow of communism, the CIA showed up in Burma to boost the Chinese Nationalists-in-exile there, the Kuomintang (KMT). The plan? To organize Burmese tribes for what would become three disastrous invasions into China.[20] Burma was the poorest of the poor highland countries, and to cope, tycoons inside the country had set up a small narcotics-based economy by pressuring peasant farmers to grow poppies. Then the KMT stepped up to the plate. In exchange for military help for its proposed take-over of Communist China, it donated mule caravans to cart morphine bricks out of mountain isolation south into Thailand. There the bricks underwent chemical processing, and the resulting heroin was transported to Bangkok for sale.

With access to previously unreachable Southeast Asian markets, and eventually to European and American consumers, Burma's opium production grew 500 percent — from less than eighty tons a year after World War II to 400 tons by the mid-1960s — to become the largest opium-growing region in the world.[21]

The right hand and the left. "No" was the word the US government pressed upon France and Turkey; "Yes" was its nod to Southeast Asia. The CIA was hooked up with the merging traffic on two counts — it supported the KMT's efforts to invade China by providing arms, equipment, and money;[22] and General Phao Siyanan, who graciously received the morphine in Thailand and sent it on to Bangkok, was sitting fat in his khakis on the CIA payroll.[23]

Laos-Thailand-Hong Kong. The Vietnam war was raging. Because of political infighting stemming from various Mafia-launched subterfuges against their operations, the Corsicans gave up flying the hill-grown opium of another struggling-to-survive tribe, the Laotian Hmong, to factories in Hong Kong. The CIA jumped in like a vulture, using its own Air America to transport bundles of raw opium from remote villages in the north to waiting refineries in Hong Kong — and to waiting addicts in what soon became the city with the most per-capita drug users in the world: 100,000 out of 4 million people.[24] With this help the Hmong were able to survive on their cash crop, and in exchange they gave the US what it wanted: an army of 30,000, mostly adolescent boys, to monitor US radar installations along the North Vietnam border.[25]

In 1971 the CIA made a revealing admission: one-third of the refineries in the Golden Triangle were producing not the lower-grade no. 3 that locals used, but rather the expensive, ultra-refined no. 4 preferred by American addicts.[26] The largest factory was situated in Laos. Curiously, as part of his effort at modernization-a-la-corporate-development termed "Vietnamization," President Nixon had been the #1 promoter of its construction. But the "Pepsi Cola" plant never did produce a bottle of soda. What it produced went to a cluster of sniffers and shooters who indeed had come to appreciate no. 4: US GIs in Vietnam.[27]

No. 4/Double UO Globe. Fine, bitter, and soluble. 80-99 percent pure, top-of-the-line. No. 4 is made by heating equal amounts of acetic anhydride and morphine until they bond into diacetylmorphine. Dissolve the impurities by cleaning the granules in a solution of water and chloroform, then with activated charcoal. Add ether and hydrochloric acid. Tiny white flakes form. Filter them out. Ready to meet the Dragon? Heat in a steel cooking pot and pour into a syringe with saline. Inject.

I don't mean to be disrespectful. But there are only so many gold neck chains, private zoological gardens, and ten-bedroom beach houses one cartel can own. Where did the rest of the drug money go in the 1970s? It certainly wasn't visible to the naked eye.

Or was it ... and we just didn't *see*?

This is just a question, although I do speak from the personal experience of having lived through those years. How was it that so many oil pipelines, automobile factories, and luxury resorts got going back then?

Laos-Thailand-Saigon. As of 1968, American soldiers did not have a heroin problem; sales in Saigon went to local users. But in the spring of 1970, Vietnamization kicked in. The US-sponsored program poured money into South Vietnam — take note: the Hong Kong office

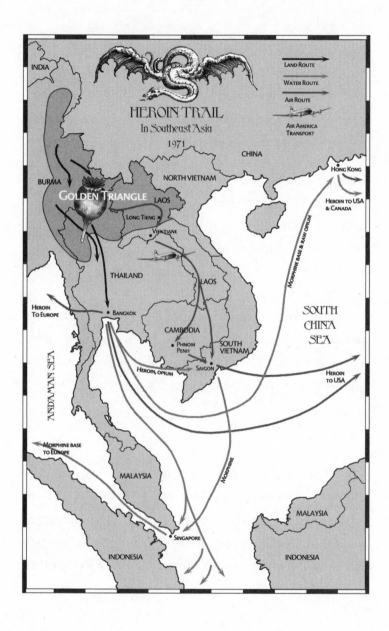

of the project was run by a Trafficante man — and the very South Vietnamese government, army, and police officials milking all that US taxpayer largesse had come up with an idea for raking in more. They used it to move heroin to GIs, beginning with what has become the standby of the manufacture of consumption — the free giveaway.[28] Young men and women lured by a need for distraction often became hooked, and by 1973 White House estimates, 34 percent of American soldiers in Vietnam — 80,000 — were using.[29]

A second new market for Southeast Asian heroin was made up of Americans too — at home. GIs were bringing the stuff back to the states.[30] It came stashed in body bags on army transport. It came via the air force postal system. It came in duffle bags. It came in balloons inside soldiers' guts.

Saigon to Oakland. To Seattle. Los Angeles.

And when the number of troops in Vietnam declined in the early '70s, it came via the Chinese and struggling-to-survive Corsican syndicates shipping Laotian heroin directly to the US.[31] And it came via the irrepressible American Mafiosos who, with the fall of Turkey and Marseilles, had rushed to pick up the slack by garnering new sources in Southeast Asia and seeding new markets in Europe and the US.[32]

By the time Joaquin was poking his young veins with a hypodermic needle, a courier ring was importing heroin along the channels Santo Trafficante and his Mafioso sidekicks had laid out. From Hong Kong the drug was flown on commercial flights to Chile, then smuggled by private aircraft across the border to Paraguay. From there it made its way north in private planes or stuffed inside mailed packages of archaeological artifacts.[33]

By 1972, 70 percent of the world's illicit opium supply was growing in the highlands of the Golden Triangle[34] — and it was getting out. Via Bangkok, Hong Kong, Saigon. To New York and Miami. London, Paris, and Amsterdam. To Chicago. To Boyle Heights.

And Chimayó.

But then again. By the time Joaquin was stabbing his arm — by the time he was hot-wiring cars on the streets of LA and making runs to poppy plantations in Sonora — Mexico had increased its share of the US market to a whopping 39 percent.[35] It's highly possible that Joaquin's first hit came from Mexico.

The sudden growth in commercial success was not merely the result of a renewed spirit among Mexican growers, entrepreneurs, and in-cahoots government officials. Surely they were trying. But no. This instance of exploding commerce came down to a reconfiguration in the patterns of global trafficking, and it shows how quickly the business can run after money.

In 1972 Thailand was a crucial springboard for shipment out of Southeast Asia — and so Thailand became the place the US Drug Enforcement Administration targeted for interdiction.[36] The agency upped the number of narcs from two to thirty-one,[37] spent $12 million to aid local police,[38] placed intelligence in the region's biggest ports — Hong Kong, Bangkok, and Manila — and intercepted shipments destined for the states.[39] The result: by 1975 SE Asian heroin — so plentiful during the heyday of the Vietnam War — had dropped to a mere 9 percent of the total seized inside the United States.[40]

As Alfred McCoy tells it, while this campaign was successful, it had unintended side effects. He uses the metaphor of the sorcerer's apprentice. US interdiction in Thailand encouraged a global scattering of what had previously been a centralized, and therefore knowable business. Smaller cartels sprung up like magic brooms, making efforts at suppression next-to-impossible and contributing to an increase in consumers in both the

US and Europe. By 1975 — when the Vietnam War ended and SE Asian heroin was on the wane — Mexico had come, ever so momentarily, to supply 90 percent of the US market.[41]

And now Joaquin was shooting it in his cell at Soledad prison.

Black Tar/Mexican Mud. Brown and gummy like roofing pitch. 2-10 percent pure. This is the castoff crud from the chemical process of refining no. 4, what they use to feed the dogs. Place a lump in a sawed-off soda can. Drop a lump on a tear of aluminum foil. Whichever. Heat from below with a Bic lighter. Pour into a syringe with salt solution.

1989: Joaquin is meticulous about one thing. *Chiva.* He is crouched on his knees on the dirt floor of the Cruz family homestead in Chimayó, leaning over the coffee table ever so precisely packaging Black Tar from plastic casing into BBs and balloons.

He has meticulously sold almost everything in the house to support his habit — refrigerator, cook stove, overhead lamps, firewood, sinks, boom box, light bulbs, front-door lock, the silver shirt his father gave him back in 1957. He has even dug up the floors of the back rooms with a pick axe to unload the iron plumbing pipes for cash. And his father and mother have long since sold the chile field and irrigation rights to pay for Joaquin's parade of lawyers.

He nods out over the coffee table, and meticulousness is lost. A wind picks up outside, blows cold spring air through the shattered glass of the front window, and a '77 Barracuda pulls up under the cottonwood tree. When Joaquin wakes up, all the bags and all the balloons are gone.

Chances are pretty good that the *chiva* lifted from Joaquin's living room came from the Golden Triangle. The year was 1989, and production in Burma had resurged. The area as a whole was growing 72 percent of the world's illicit supply [42] and 80 percent of the catch for New York City.[43] Chances are even better that the bags and balloons that disappeared came from Mexico, whose business waxed and waned depending on weather, interdiction efforts, and the vagaries of the syndicates. Although Mexico was growing less than 1 percent of the world market,[44] it was right across the border — and putting out a new-and-improved Black Tar that combined high purity with low price.[45]

But chances are good too that Joaquin's stolen cache came from Afghanistan via Pakistan, a route that was fast providing heroin to most of Europe and nearly half of America's 700,000 addicts.[46]

Afghanistan. It's the same triangulated story. *Third World military-government honchos moonlighting as drug traffickers; desperate peasant peoples forced to grow narcotics instead of food; and the US government — all played out within the context of capitalism's urgency to crush competing systems.*

Throughout the 1970s opium use in Iran, Pakistan, and Afghanistan was small-scale and self-contained. A convergence of events led to a change. To begin, there was a drought that demolished the Golden Triangle's crop for two years running. Then, in 1979, the Ayatollah's Islamic regime came into power in Iran, supplanting the formerly US-friendly government with a flare of anti-American fist-shaking. In the face of such a challenge, the US's propensity to anti-drug grandstanding resurfaced like an old chancre; we demanded that neighboring Pakistan suppress its crops to cut off Iran's source. As Pakistan's harvest dried up, tribal farmers across the border in Afghanistan saw the opportunity and expanded the fields they had previously grown for local use. Most critically, the Soviet army invaded the Hindu Kushi mountains in a last-ditch Cold War effort to seize Afghanistan's potential oil-pipeline lands and military-base terrain.

Enter the Central Intelligence Agency.

The CIA immediately began working with Pakistani intelligence to train, arm, and launch the first anti-communist resistance troops from among these same drug-growing tribesmen. It was the agency's largest covert operation yet. Pouring $3 billion into the ten-year war, the US set up ultra-high-tech electronic surveillance systems and made daily reconnaissance flights with F-16 fighter planes. The anti-Soviet guerrillas, coalescing under the banner of the Taliban, received another $2 billion in covert aid from the CIA.[47] They used the money to capture the richest agricultural lands in the nation — not to grow food for the Afghani people, but to grow opium. Operating under a veil of military protection, the guerrilla-traffickers were able to transport their harvest to an estimated 200 heroin labs at the Afghan-Pakistani border in the same military vehicles that were trucking in American arms.[48] They then used their new international contacts to peddle their drugs inside Pakistan, where addiction suddenly rocketed — from 5,000 users in 1980 to 1.3 million by 1986.[49] They moved in on Soviet soldiers as a ploy to weaken the enemy, using the tried-and-true free giveaway.[50] Finally, the new Afghani traffickers sold heroin to dealers who transported the stuff to Europe and the US.

The result was a ten-fold explosion of production inside Afghanistan, from 200 tons in 1981 to 2,000 tons in 1990.[51] By the mid-1990s, the Golden Crescent of South Asia was supplying 70 percent of the world's heroin,[52] 60 percent of which was being shipped to the United States.[53]

The question doesn't go away. Where does all the profit go?

When you hang around the bait box at the general store in Chimayó, you hear things. You might hear that some businessmen in Española are the undercover bucks behind the local drug trade. You might hear that a warehouse outside Las Vegas, New Mexico, harbors a three-month back-up supply. Or that a high-level meeting to plan regional distribution takes place at a ranch in Sapello. Or there's a landing strip on a ridge above Abiquiú.

Whatever.

The only thing that really matters now is that Joaquin doesn't have a single balloon to sell. Worse, he doesn't have any to inject.

The inclination. It explodes like a star being born in a black sky. The temptation. It expands at the edges. The urge. The craving. The need. The lust. It shivers across half the sky. The necessity. The greed. The obsession. It becomes everything: earth air water body world *everything*.

Joaquin begins to sweat, first around his armpits and into the seams of his Levi shirt. The flush surges into his neck and ears, then burns down his chest and spine. He rips the wet shirt from his torso. He is hot as hell. Then, suddenly, a pierce of icy pain shoots over his left hip and down his leg. It is metallic like the cold stab of a spike, and in response his toes cramp into twisted forms resembling frozen tree roots.

With the effort of a maimed dragon, Joaquin hauls himself across the mud floor, along the way bunching up the smelly shag rug into a wad of tentacles around his thighs. He kicks the door open. The wind outside is howling, and a few solo snowflakes nose-dive to the ground. Abruptly, Joaquin's bowels let loose like a sewer tap, and he fills his icy pants with hot muck. Undeterred, he rolls himself into the door jam — the fire of his upper body smoldering now in the cold air; his freezing, feculent legs swaddled in shag in the relative warmth of the house.

# IV.

We are well into Lent now. It's late February, the time of year set aside for reflection and sacrifice. Quite a few people in Chimayó renounce Bud Light for the duration. Others give up dancing at the casino, and while the pilgrims will not begin to make their offering for another month or so, there is a feeling of expectancy along the roads leading into the village.

You might say that it's odd, this trekking across the desert to a mud church. You might ask: how many thousands upon thousands of feet have laid imprint to the sand along these roads? How many millions of praises have been sung? How many prayers whispered? And yet, despite it all, Chimayó suffers. The entire Española valley suffers. Northern New Mexico suffers. A dancer with Danza Azteca de Anáhuac named Linda Velarde holds firm on the connection between the depth of one's faith and real-world results. "Heroin is eating up our men, our children, our way of life," she insists. "We aren't mustering enough faith. When we walk, we have to do better."[54]

I would be the first to have faith in faith. Think of the Africans shackled to iron rings in the bellies of slave ships. Think of Mahatma Gandhi. Nelson Mandela. For that matter, think of Joaquin Cruz. How did they endure the anguish? Certainly persistence is required if we are to survive the terrible twists and turns that warp the world today. Faith is required if we are to survive with integrity. Yet maybe, along with these strengths, we also need to ground ourselves in how things came to be as they are. Maybe historical perspective is in order.

Where did heroin come from?

Opium. The sticky brown sap lanced from the head of the poppy. 3-17 percent pure. Dissolve the sap in boiling water, and strain out the soil and twigs. Then reheat until the water evaporates. Dry. Place in a pipe. Light with a stick of incense. Lie down and inhale.

Opium comes from the *Papaver somniferum* plant, which was grown and used as a medicine in the eastern Mediterranean as far back as 2500 BCE, just as *ayahuasca* has been used in the Amazon rainforest, *iboga* in west Africa, and the coca leaf in the Andes highlands. Hippocrates is on record recommending a drink made of white poppy juice and nettle seed in the 4th century BCE. By 800 CE use of opium had spread across the breadth of Asia from modern-day Turkey to southeastern Asia — as a regionally-traded folk remedy, not an internationally sought-after capitalist commodity. That change in status came in the 17th century when European empires began to insert their global strategies into Asian trade.

The critical component of opium sap was morphine, an alkaloid whose power to numb pain and bring on sleep came intertwined with an extraordinary imposition of addiction.

Morphine. *Pi-tzu* in Chinese. Coffee-colored and coarse. Stir prepared opium into a brew of hot water and lime fertilizer. When the morphine floats to the top, filter it out, and heat a second time with ammonium chloride. What you're looking for drops to the bottom in chunks.

Morphine in its pure form was separated from opium sap in 1803. German pharmacist assistant Friedrich Wilhelm Sertürner first isolated the crystal salt in a home experiment. He wanted to see what this new substance would do, so he talked three friends into ingesting it. Almost immediately the men doubled over with agonizing cramps and headaches. Sertürner gave them an antidote, and they threw up and fell into profound sleep.[55]

1853. Two separate doctors — Scotsman Alexander Wood and Charles Gabriel Pravaz from France — invented the hypodermic syringe with its hollow needle. Its first use was to inject morphine as a painkiller. Twenty-one years later, in 1874, a chemist at St. Mary's Hospital in London took the inventive process one step further: he synthesized heroin from morphine. C.R. Alder Wright had in mind to separate the addictive element of morphine from its therapeutic essence, and he attempted this by heating it with acetic anhydride, filtering the product, heating it again and filtering it again. When ingested, the grainy powder that resulted caused prostration, fear, vomiting, diminished heart rate, sweating, itchiness, shortness of breath, loss of coordination, and sleepiness — or, as reported from inside the experience, an altered state of consciousness.

1898. The Bayer Company of Germany had two new compounds to choose from: aspirin and this new derivative of morphine. Of the former they proclaimed, "The product is worthless!" They proceeded to export the latter to twenty-three countries amid the hoopla of an ad campaign claiming it was a wonder drug for coughing, chest pain, pneumonia, and TB — and could even be used to beat off morphine addiction.

Bayer called the new product heroin for the German word *heroisch*, or "heroic."

People have used extraordinary means to achieve altered states of consciousness for as long as we have existed. Chanting. Dancing. Fasting. Subjecting one's body to heat. Subjecting one's body to cold. Going to sleep. Staying awake. Breathing fast. Breathing slow. Consuming plant medicine. When explored within a container of ceremonial rites, altered states have been crucial to humanity for their contributions to individual development, collective survival, and species evolution. It is only in recent times, with the dissociation of experience and thought produced by mass society, that the powers of altered states have been pursued arhythmically from season and outside their place within ceremony.

Knowing the story of the British is critical to understanding where the heroin in our midst originates. The famed empire began its world-hungry exploits during the Age of Exploration when, in the 15th and 16th centuries, cartographers and sailors launched their endeavors of expansive curiosity. Then came Britain's realization of cruel possibility: the Time of Taking. Australia. New Zealand. New Guinea. Ceylon. Hong Kong. Malaysia. The Asian subcontinent. The Middle East. East Africa from Egypt to South Africa. Guiana. The Caribbean. Ireland. Canada. All of which lay the groundwork for 1914, when England, along with the other European nations, held title to 85 percent of the planet's landmass.[56]

Curiously, the opium poppy laid the base for the whole operation.

I pull up to Orlando's, and the *viejo* wiping his windshield with a bandana at the next pump calls over to me. "*¿Sabes como* it used to be?" he enunciates across the rusting hood of a '55 Apache. I am in for a history lesson. Or shall I say, *another* history lesson, for in these parts history is spoken all the time.

"How did it used to be, sir?"

"It used to be that the men went into the forest to be men. *Pá cazar y pescar y coger la leña. Entonces venían los norteamericanos.* Y they outright stole the land. Now that same stealing is running around all *chiva chingada* inside the veins of the men."

It used to be that, before colonization by the US in 1848, the men had a job to do and the freedom with which to do it. Robert Bly, you fox! The scenario of male wounding in northern New Mexico echoes that which the poet-philosopher describes in his writings about European and American men at the time of the industrial revolution.[57] As empire-building and industrialism merged to create mass society, the men were routed off the land — away from hunting and fishing and gathering wood — into task-mastered jobs with no apparent relationship to real-world survival. And in most cases, with no freedom. The psychic outcome of this social disruption was the kind of disembodiment, repression, and disorientation we find seething within men today.

One difference between men long-assimilated into mass society and those in the villages of northern New Mexico is that *norteños* do not need an academic to fill in the blanks of lost memory. They know their history.

Their fathers and grandfathers have told them all along, just as I am told over a Chevy hood at Orlando's general store. And they can see for themselves. The men of *el norte* still live in the land of the *antepasados*. The very forests that fed their ancestors, built their villages, sustained their culture — and were then commandeered by the US government — are right here. The elk are here. The trout are here. The ponderosa are here. But the men cannot get into the forests that were once theirs, *las mercedes* or land grants, without enduring an unceasing requirement for certification, permitting, licensing ... and cash. As they mark time in lines at the government offices down in Santa Fe, eyes cast toward a waxed floor, their bones are the thing to silently scream the injustice, the violence, the forked tongue that wrested from them their cherished place on this Earth.

Enter a euphoria-inducing drug. Like a heroine. *La puta*, they call it. The mistress.

"What was it that did in reality make me an opium-eater?" wrote Thomas DeQuincey in 1821. "That affection which finally drove me into the habitual use of opium, what was it? Pain was it? No, but misery. Casual overcasting of sunshine was it? No, but blank desolation. Gloom was it that might have departed? No, but settled and abiding darkness."[58]

The story of heroin is an abidingly dark tale of ellipsus. Track your finger along the cusp of a mobius strip. It just keeps going around and around and around. Like the arm of Joaquin's neighbor in East LA.

To sustain the original act of theft, a reorganization of land-based community becomes necessary: colonization is required. *Local men are torn from their nature-based livelihoods and forced to act as wage-slaves for mass production in the newly-constructed nation-state.* The anguish this condition provokes, if felt, is more than a man can bear. And if it does find its way to expression, its display can bring more anguish in the form of punishment. Hence, the need to quell feeling.

The British had this all figured out. Their Golden Triangle became the most profitable route to amass

capital for an empire in the history of the world —
and it all began with opium.

The green hills and rich valleys of India's Bengal
state were perfect for growing narcotics. The Queen's
men forced the locals to disband small-scale food and
cotton farming to grow the commodity crop. Wielding
muskets, they made them lance the poppy, scrape
away the sap, and dry it into transportable balls. The
executors of the British East India Company master-
minded the economics of the endeavor. But there was
a glitch. Hindu culture did not lend itself to drug
abuse, and so they instructed the locals to pack the
harvest into wooden chests, each containing forty balls
and weighing 140 pounds.[59] Iron frigates, and later
clipper ships, carried the precious cargo across the
China Sea to coastal cities like Kwangchow (Canton)
and Hangchow (Hangchou). There they pioneered
what became the accepted method for creating consumption; they gave the drug away in the streets and,
to service the made-to-order population of addicts,
connived with local businessmen to establish special
dens for sales and use, what we call shooting galleries.

Business mushroomed. In 1770 only fifteen metric
tons of opium was making the trip across the sea; by

1906 the total had soared to 39,000 tons — with 13.5 million addicts in China, or 27 percent of the adult male population.[60]

With the spectacular 2,600-fold profit generated by this early stab at global marketing, English entrepreneurs bought up Chinese teas, silks, and porcelains and shipped them to Europe. The rich and royal ate up the exotic fineries, of course — but the nouveau class of mid-level brokers and service-providers did as well. Middle class sensibility was given its contents: the department store was born, and money was amassed hand over fist over bank account. Then, British East India turned its attention back to the original source of all this profit-taking. Bereft of the cotton crops they had once spun and weaved for themselves, Indian people were pressed to buy the textiles now being assembled in Great Britain's new factories from cotton grown on wage-slave plantations in ... India.

The wealth this triangle of trade amassed jump-started the very industrial revolution Robert Bly bemoans for its wrenching of man from land in Europe. It financed the Royal Navy, the model for militarizing the male psyche into assembly-line obedience, and the navy's task became to capture more land

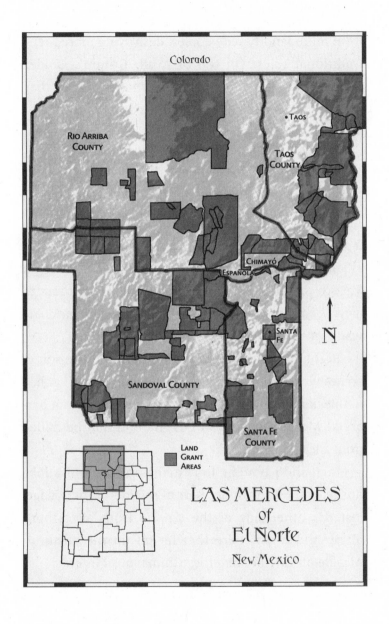

Colorado

• Taos

Rio Arriba County

Taos County

Chimayó

Española

Santa Fe

N

Sandoval County

Santa Fe County

Land Grant Areas

LAS MERCEDES
of
El Norte
New Mexico

from more land-based peoples, destroying more men's traditional roles. On top of it all, Britain's Golden Triangle gave birth to mass production of a drug that, on the surface, alleviated the very agonies caused by all this stress — and to mass addiction to that drug among men.

It's not a big challenge to create "mass" addiction in a village. Abuse of *chiva* spread across northern New Mexico the same way it spreads through any community: *somebody gives it out* — and then sits back and waits for the customers.

Right after the Vietnam War, one of those somebodies was a *vato* named Luis Vialpando. The man had jet-black hair and a face like an Indian. He was a barber at Mr. Topper's up in Los Alamos, and he hailed from Alcalde.

Vialpando bought four acres and an old adobe house in the Rincón del Barrial section of the village, just the other side of the *acequia* from his father's place, and it was here that he set up the business. Alcalde quickly became the "Chimayó" of its era.

Then, over in Dixon, he fixed up his mother's adobe to look like a barber shop. The place came to be known as "*la clinica*," and all the low-riders and teenagers hung out and got high. This wasn't a trifling effort, mind you; the stuff came in by helicopter, reportedly at 4 a.m., reportedly from Denver, and it fanned out from there to Velarde, Española, Córdova, and Chimayó.[61] There was also a firing range in an *arroyo* where the guys could practice using machine guns that — one can only guess — were vintage-Vietnam.

Robberies overtook Alcalde and Dixon like an outbreak of pimples. A Catholic nun was attacked at the convent in San Juan Pueblo. And legend has it that when Vialpando got hauled off to the state pen, what's known as the Balloon Effect emerged: press on the surface of a balloon in one place, it bulges in another. The new hub of trade protruded across the valley from Alcalde and an easy pickup-truck ride down the road from Dixon ... in Chimayó.

If you met Joaquin, you might be impressed by his intelligence. If you spent time with him, perhaps walked to *la presa*, angled together for some *truchas* on the river, if you cooked up your catch along with some wild *kelites* and made conversation beneath the Sangre de Cristo stars, you might regard him as a man of sensitivity.

He started tear-assing into banks in East LA at the age of nineteen. His first gun was a snub-nose Star .38. He found it under a lemon tree outside the Gomez house that night the LAPD raided and the *vatos* with their balloons of *chiva* scattered in a panic. As Joaquin was running, about three blocks from the house, the metal of the discarded gun's barrel caught the glare of a streetlamp, sending out a single beam of light. Joaquin froze in his tracks. He threw his heaving body behind an oleander bush and then, gathering himself like a hunter in his grandfather's forest, pounced upon his prey.

It came in handy when he joined up with Ricky Razo to take that first bank on Hollywood Boulevard. The two wore sports jackets they'd picked up at the Goodwill, light-colored to avoid notice. They parked Joaquin's father's "borrowed" Fairlane right in front of the bank, keys still dangling from the ignition. Ricky went in first and staked out the guards. Joaquin straggled behind looking nonchalant, stood in line — there were only two people ahead of him — and then ambled up to the teller. *"Buenos días,"* he offered. "You look nice today." Then he pressed a note into her hand and signaled with his eyes that he was clutching a gun under his breast pocket. She swept all her cash into a canvas bag and pushed it toward him. Joaquin and Ricky walked out and drove away.

It was as simple as that. So simple they did it again and again — in the process trying out new variations in their routine (locking all the customers, guards, and tellers in the vault was one) and applying their expertise at *suavísimo* toward whole wardrobes (polyester suits, penny loafers, tennis wear) that mimicked their study of American respectability.

In district court, as World-War-II veteran Mr. Cruz fought off a rash of prickles across his neck, Joaquin faced what turned out to be a not-difficult choice. "You can either serve in Vietnam," proclaimed the judge. "Or you can spend the next two years at Soledad." Joaquin did not look at his father, and he did not flinch in his answer. "I take *la pinta*," he said. "At least there I know who is the enemy."

The naivete of the twenty-year-old! Truth is, in prison you don't necessarily know who your enemy is. To begin with, you can get *chiva* on the inside like candy from a vending machine. It's no surprise: 73 percent of federal prisoners have used drugs, and more than two-thirds were trafficking during the offense that landed them behind bars.[62] Given the uncertainties of alliance that fester in the presence of drugs, you best get hooked up with one of the brotherhoods that rule on the inside. Joaquin walked right from the mugshot room into his *barrio*'s birthright, a pack made of the bros he knew from Boyle Heights.

He would need them.

There were these twins, you see. They were white boys, hairy, rough-mouthed, and they hung together. After Joaquin had been at Soledad for not yet a week, the twins cornered him in the yard. Standing side-by-side like a police sweep, they pushed him beyond the open space into a corner. "Hey, Mexican candy-ass! Take your pants off!" snarled the one as the other made a lunge for Joaquin's balls. Like a flash he reached into his sock and pulled out the six-inch machine-shop shank the *vatos* had given him. He stabbed at the twins in an airy slash and, at the moment of their surprise, darted between them toward the immediate safety of the yard.

It was his ability to dart that gave Joaquin value in prison. He could suck all the life out of his limbs and, like a tai chi master, congeal it right in the center of his being. Then, nearly invisible, he could move as quick as a jackrabbit. The arrangement with the prison guards helped. In exchange for cash or heroin, depending on their proclivities, the guards let Joaquin slip into the parking lot, to the edges of allowed space, to procure the pick-up from the outside. Then they let him roam throughout the prison making deliveries — from the "mainline" corridor where inmates gathered when not in their cells to the despised X and O wings known as "the Hole." In his job as drug runner, Joaquin was not a candy-ass.

And he was well rewarded for his stealth. The bros gave him protection against hostile gangs, vengeful guards, and the twins. He did indeed come to know who was the enemy, but the lines of demarcation were not simple and were never drawn according to role.

The *vatos* also rewarded him with syringes, cookers, matches, and *chiva*, as much as he craved, and when he wasn't tracking its delivery and distribution, he was tracking his arm. It was that or go mad. The windowless 10-by-10 cell crammed with mattress, wash bowl, and toilet was more like a 6-by-6 vault. In it, either Joaquin went crazy with the incessant if-only's and could-have-been's that fused with the desperation, hate, and despair already encrusted in the subterranean passageways of his psyche.

Or he shot up.

The Dragon makes an appearance in the dream world. Fabulous Dragon. Fleet-footed. Fiery. Animal of animals: eagle, crocodile, and lion combined.

The Dragon rises up something terrible from behind the altar at Holy Family parish in Boyle Heights, the heavy air of the nave suddenly churning in seering gusts. The people in the pews scream, jump up, and cram out the front doors in a stampede like a zoot suit riot. Joaquin is pushed through the portal in a scuffle of patent leather shoes and flailing shirt sleeves. Then, mightily holding his position against the force of the crowd, he freezes. Inside a cloud of self-willed calm, he gazes down at the stone step. A cockroach appears: it is in danger of being trampled. Joaquin bends down to shield the spindly creature from the frantic footfall of human-made soles.

Then he looks up. The scene of chaos is gone. There are no more church steps. No more terrified crowd. No more screaming and panic. He is a boy in Chimayó, the air caressing his summer-tan skin, the *acequia* streaming by, and the beast has shape-shifted into a sheepdog.

Joaquin jerks awake. His left arm aches like a cottonwood branch chain-sawed from its trunk. He rolls over in his prison cot and adjusts his eyes. On his arm, across the soft skin of the inside bend, he finds a tattoo etched in blue India ink, the image of a fierce wild beast: a Dragon.

# V.

Fierce, wild beasts elicit three kinds of response. The first, understandably, is to run. Heroin houses! Knifings! Ex-cons! Some people from the valley flee down the Río Grande to Albuquerque, away from the dastardly maneuvers of dealers and addicts, toward the ways of survival offered up by the urban world. (What is called 'Burque is, of course, a hub of drug trafficking in its own right, but in cities, after all, illusion prevails.) Flight by omission is another way to run. Out of sight, as they say. When I moved to Chimayó, Anglos from the seeming safety of other places skipped the celebration for a woman's success at purchasing a house and cut right to their fears. Was I going to leave? they pressed. Flee from the beast? they pleaded. Do them the favor of removing Chimayó from their minds?

When you are rooted in the land, though, you do not run. Such is the response of native peoples. The land is contaminated by radiation from aboveground nuclear testing; the people do not leave. The community is cut in two by a six-lane freeway; the people make no departure. The river dries up from global warming; they stay. The people and the land are one: they made of the land, the land made of them. So it is for the Chicanos of northern New Mexico. For all the ones who flee, there are others for whom leaving is not a thought.

A second reaction to beasts is to muster your resources and fight. Across history and around the world, the Dragon is the mythic characterization of wildness and volatility — read: the Enemy — because within societies that cultivate separation, order, and discipline in pursuit of survival, such qualities must be beaten back by heroic slayers.

But wait. The British East India Company did not pursue police action to quell drug users. Au contraire, the company's wealth was *based* on its monopoly over what was, at the time, a legal narcotics trade. It was only when profits fell into competing hands, and when the effects of mass addiction grew too appalling for the socially-concerned that prohibition and policing became the primary weapons for taming the beast. In 1923, after some thirty years of groundwork by Christian believers, medical doctors, and elected officials exposing the dependency-inducing properties of heroin (and cocaine), the first US drug agency was established. On the international front, the Geneva Convention of 1925 and the Limitation Convention of 1931 imposed strict regulations on the production and export of legal opiates, all but terminating their flow. In response, criminal networks arose to fill the demand for what was now illicit and, particularly during the intensity of 1920s Prohibition, they mushroomed in size, power, and capital. To counter these developments, policing agencies themselves ballooned, and the dynamic between the two became the modern-day battle between Archangel St. Michael's fighting units and the scaly Dragon of addicts and pushers. It also became the reason for governments to slap the "Just Say No" card onto the table — all the while arranging under-the-table deals with politically-*simpatico* narco-dealers.

Linda Pedro came upon a third approach to address northern New Mexico's bestiary: faith. Envelop the creature in beauty, she proposed. Transform it by recreating its environment. Ease it toward its true place. Her vision was to stage a most unusual pilgrimage to the Santuario — right through the heart of the dealers' domain.

Pedro was a fact of life in Chimayó. Born to a Mexican mother and a Scottish labor-organizer father, she had lived in her three-room adobe house for thirty-five years. Disabled since 1966, she was bound to a wheelchair and welfare. A grandmother and deeply spiritual woman, she resided at the center of a swirl of goodness — sweat lodges, summer parties, equinox celebrations, *horno* oven bakes — just as she resided in the dark swirl of the incessant comings-and-goings, fist fights, and gunshots occurring right next door at Fat José Martinez's heroin *tiendita*.

The idea for a procession sprang from a serendipitous meeting at the Stroke and Rehabilitation Center in Española. The year was 1997. A funeral reception was in full and sober swing in the entrance area when Linda wheeled herself across the linoleum, headed for the physical therapy room. An hour later she reemerged, and the room was stone empty — except for two women silently sponging down the tables. Pedro introduced herself. The older woman asked why she was in a wheelchair. Pedro explained that she had been in a car accident. The younger woman blurted out that her daughter, for whom the funeral was held, had been killed in a car accident. The incident was known to us all. A young man had plied some high school students with alcohol and drugs and, careening down Route 76, missed the curve at the post office. Three young corpses lay strewn across the tar. The woman fell sobbing into Pedro's arms.

Unable to shake the agony and poignancy of this encounter, she asked herself, "What in God's world can I do about this tragedy?" Then she asked the question again. And again. And again. At night, in the flicker of candles surrounding her plaster-of-paris statue of the Guadalupe, she journeyed deep inside to pray for a sign.

It was there in the silence of spirit that she heard the voices of her ancestors. They spoke of a pilgrimage to the Santuario focused on the drug epidemic. According to Chicano tradition, such a procession could initiate a communal "taking back" of stolen space. Then the *antepasados* reminded her: in the old days, when things weren't going well in the village, the grandmothers looked to the Hermanos for help.

Joaquin was the first to tell me about the Hermanos. His father had been one, and it would have been his legacy to join the order, had he not been in and out of prison. Once, at Christmas time, he squired me to the edges of a ceremony beginning in a mud hovel of a *morada* and proceeding down a dirt road, across the *arroyo*, and through the village, all the while emanating the magnificently manly tones of traditional chants.

La Fraternidad Piadosa de Nuestro Padre Jesús Nazareno is an all-male religious order that arose in northern New Mexico in the late 1700s when Spain's Catholic Church, headquartered a full three-days' burro ride south in Santa Fe, could not administer to or control its far-flung colonies to the north. Modeling their rites after traditional Spanish mystical practices adapted to native conditions, the part-Hispano/part-indigenous men filled the spiritual vacuum, providing leadership and aid to their communities. Then, starting in the mid-1800s, the archbishops of the Catholic Church curtailed the men's activities, and a new wrinkle to the male experience of colonization appeared. To survive the hostility, the Hermanos went underground.

Pedro approached them in that place. Underground. It was one cold November night when the cottonwood branches were sheathed in ice. Faraway stars broadcast the only glisten in a black sky, and she secretly invited a few men she knew to be Hermanos to her home. There by the fire she made an unusual and, for a woman and non-member, startling request. "I am speaking to you as a grandmother from the village," she said. "I'm asking you to remember who you are. We're losing our children. Can you lead the way?"

It took over a year for them to respond. To consider breaking from the rite of secrecy they had protected, and that had protected them, would require a drawn-out process of consensual thinking involving each of the more than 100 *moradas* in New Mexico. But the request, as the Hermanos saw it, asked a far thornier question than merely whether to participate or not. The question was whether they were ready: was each member of the order *himself* free of substance abuse?

Pedro did not know why they were taking so long. As she waited she began, tentatively, to contact other possible participants. Every phone call was an effort. She would corral the receiver against the bedspread with her hands the way someone else might while wearing potholder gloves. Then she pressed the buttons with either the side of her thumb or a knuckle and, as the phone rang at the other end, maneuvered the receiver up her arm to a nest between her shoulder and ear. She spoke to mothers of children who had been killed by both participation in the heroin trade or as innocent victims of the violence it generated. She drew in leaders of all faiths practiced in the valley. She garnered the organizing expertise of crucial local agencies like Río Arriba Family Care Network and Española Crisis Center, tribal organizations like Eight Northern Indian Pueblo Council, and grassroots groups like the brand-new Chimayó Crime Prevention Organization. Its focus paralleled Pedro's, but its method was to catalyze cooperation between the New Mexico State

Police and federal agencies like the FBI and DEA, while siphoning information and evidence to them. Pedro got everything poised for the go-ahead. Then she parked her wheelchair next to the Guadalupe. And she prayed.

Winter passed. Spring splattered us with mud and blew our cowboy hats off. Summer blossomed. Autumn. Then the snows dusted the Sangre de Cristo mountains once again.

Joaquin's seasons were also passing. He would be just fine, thriving in fact, for months at a time. All the while Linda Pedro was waiting for the Hermanos, he was holding down two jobs. He excelled as a substance abuse counselor at an alcohol treatment center, and he was teaching guitar. After a while his '79 Ford LTD croaked, and I would see him walking along the road to work. I pulled over sometimes. He would arise to his full five-foot-three, take my hand, bend over with much fanfare, and kiss it.

Then, out of the blue, he wasn't just fine. He was on the lam from parole, popping valium, making endless trips to 'Burque. Tommy from the Chamisa Lounge, an on-again/off-again cocaine addict himself, called to spill not only the current situation, but the underlying one. "He's gone back to his old ways," he said. Wink, wink.

By the time Pedro heard back from the Hermanos and was flying ahead with plans for the Interfaith Procession to End Violence from Drugs and Alcohol, Joaquin was crashing at his sister's house in Española and thinking rationally about his options after this latest parole violation. Sitting on the couch with a bag of tortilla chips, we were watching Spanish talent shows on Loretta's wide-screen TV, and I asked my friend to cross the line he usually toed by marching with me against drug abuse.

DULCE MARIA
DULCE MARIA
AVE MARIA
AVE MARIA

In their ragtag plastic-bag raincoats, Levi *ranchero* jackets, and tee-shirts identifying village and *morada*,

150 men from Los Hermanos Penitentes led 300 marchers the eight miles from the old adobe church of Santa Cruz to the Santuario in Chimayó. Singing from as deep in their bellies as a cave at the center of the Earth, their voices infused the entire procession with chilling solemnity. Behind them marched the families of the people who had been killed by drugs, alcohol, and the violence they inevitably spawned. Mothers, fathers, sisters, cousins — they were carrying hand-made cardboard signs with messages like "DANNY CHAVEZ, SENSELESSLY MURDERED" and "IN MEMORY OF VENESSA VALARIO." Then came the rest of us: residents of Chimayó, Truchas, Alcalde, El Rito, Peñasco, Embudo, La Madera, Hernandez, Española. We were people of all faiths — Catholic, Tewa, Jewish, Sikh, Muslim, Aztec, Pentacostal, Protestant — marching together to create a miracle.

For a Saturday morning in May, the sky was low and threatening. Torrents of rain and snow were emptying onto the upland desert to the south and east. But miraculously, no precipitation was falling along 76. The march took up a whole lane of traffic. Motorists in the opposite lane slammed on the brakes and stared. For the first time in 150 years their spiritual leaders were conducting worship in full view of the public. Middle-aged men in rusted-out pickup trucks burst into tears. Whole families spontaneously clutched one another. Old women crossed themselves.

For the first time I realized the power of the Brotherhood. I had, by 1999, lived in Chimayó for nearly a decade. Eagerly I had engaged in the many facets of its vibrant culture: its thousand-year old *acequia* system, elk and deer hunting, its impassioned *norteño* music with accordian and guitar. But the power centered in the *moradas* had been a mystery. Now, for the first time, I was given a glimpse of it.

The Penitentes bellowed, "Ave Maria, Ave Maria," as spring swallows darted from cottonwood to cottonwood, showing us the way. Bruce Richardson of Chimayó Crime Prevention hopped from discarded syringe to discarded syringe, tagging its location with neon-pink ribbon for the hazardous materials team that would follow. Just past Sombrillo, marchers handed out big buttons displaying photo images of young people who had died. Mine showed a man, about seventeen years old, wearing a suit jacket and tie: Kevin Martinez. I was familiar with the story of each death. Kevin had been killed by a drunk driver.

Erik Sanchez had been pushed off the bridge at Río Grande Gorge by drug dealers stealing his car. Nine-year old Venessa Valario had been shot point blank by a burglar who broke into her mother's trailer to steal the disposable syringes Venessa used to treat diabetes. And there were buttons for Danny Chavez and Anthony Martinez, each shot through the head in Chimayó.

As we approached my neighborhood, fear crawled up the hair on my legs like a spider. What if Brian Gallegos or one of the Barela brothers saw me? Each step forward seemed a lunatic movement toward my demise. I kept walking. Past the Bionic's low-rider shop. Past Montoya's hardware. Then I saw it: the driveways into the *tienditas* were bolted shut with rocks. The dealers had fled. Instead of *tecatos* ruling the road, we were. All along the way villagers were standing in their front yards, their heads lowered and their hands clasped in prayer. Horses that normally lay in the dust of their pastures suddenly rose, arching their necks and pawing at the earth like stallions. As we neared the seven-mile mark, a new sound erupted: the beat of a drum and wail of a flute playing "Amazing Grace," courtesy of a theater troupe visiting from Spain.

At the entrance to El Santuario, there where the *acequia* quenches the pebble-lined banks, the Aztecs stopped time with the bellow of a conch shell.

A conch shell is just about what Joaquin was hearing. No explanation for not showing at the procession. As far as I can tell it's etiquette in northern New Mexico, even when you know you can't come, to never refuse an invitation. But he did march. He marched into the Santa Fe office of his parole officer. Right before he stepped through the door, he wrung one last lung full off a Camel butt. He was scared. But he did it.

The judge was a homeboy. Funny how it goes. So was the parole officer. Three homeboys in the courtroom. One in black robes. One in Yves St. Laurent. One in jailbird orange. A roughshod triangle, to be sure — with fear, contempt, compassion, and irony zooming in all directions.

"I recommend Mr. Cruz go back to prison," said the parole officer. "Or Delancy Street." Delancy Street was a tough California-based treatment center for ex-cons. To go there was the definition of a no-nonsense sentence.

"I sentence you to finish out your parole time at Drug Court in Española," countered the judge. This was surely the lightest and most hopeful option.

"But he's got armed robbery!" pleaded the DA.

"That's the past."

I was sitting in a rickety plywood theater seat in the second row with Joaquin's mother, his Nicaraguan stepfather, and two of his sisters. As my feelings for him deepened and our lives became intertwined, I would spend quite a bit of time in that seat. The judge never failed to blow my mind. The laws he was bound to follow would seem to predispose him to cut-and-dry authoritarianism. Yet, with his Cantinflas moustache and magnanimous grasp of sociology, this judge spent his decision-making in that no-man's land between discipline and caring: not afraid to lay down the law, always looking for possibility.

Beckoned by the piercing squeal of the conch shell, we gathered in the outdoor amphitheater below the church. Possibility. From the stone altar ministers, rabbis, activists, and mothers of murdered children offered their greetings and invocations. Linda Pedro was there in her wheelchair, a canary yellow blanket covering her from chin to moccasin. Rain started to drizzle down lightly, and we huddled together beneath sheets of plastic and umbrellas.

Then Celine Martinez from Chimayó's Assembly of God Church stepped to the microphone. Celine had lost two sons to drug violence. She took a breath so monstrous it must have filled every cavity in her body. And she let it out — as a high-pitched plea directly to the Heavens. Celine shouted to the Holy Spirit to lift Evil from the villages of northern New Mexico. Her voice wrapped around our skin, jarred our bones, singed our nerves.

Just then a roar let loose from about a half mile up the canyon. In an instant a blast of wind howled like a hurricane through the amphitheater, slapping branches to the ground and flipping metal umbrella spokes inside out. We were engulfed in a furiousness of weather. Drizzle turned to drench, to downpour, then to marble-size hail — and through it all, Celine Martinez was up there shrieking her lungs out to God.

And just as suddenly as she had arrived at the podium, she waned like a crescent moon, leaving us in the muffled silence of a sprinkle.

# VI.

For months things went on as before. Dealing at the *tienditas* went on. Staggering in the *arroyos* went on. Robberies went on. In those days all a *tecato* needed to score a hit was fifteen bucks. He could slither into your yard, filch a garbage can or a shovel, even a porch bulb, and be on his way to fulfillment. As Joaquin explained it, even if what a *tecato* lifted didn't add up to much, the fact that he got anything blew such a high into his being that he was likely to act all crazy —

maybe tear-assing down the road at seventy miles per hour, maybe talking loud at the *cantina*. After the procession, a lot of guys were still tear-assing and talking loud.

But then a tremor shuddered through the village like a dog flapping the river off its body. On September 13, a Chimayoso named Nicky Córdova was found in his house a few fields south of the Holy Family Church, crumpled over a pool of his own blood. Nicky was a known dealer — he was awaiting arraignment on trafficking charges — and now his body was punctured in thirty-two places, his ear sliced off and missing. Some believed the murder was a "cut off" killing perpetrated by other dealers trying to prevent incriminating testimony.

The usual somber fanfare followed. Black squad cars. Flashing red and yellow lights. The EMS van. Neighbors standing around like dusk at the edges. The next few days ushered in the aforementioned tremor, and it was made all the worse by the awkward coincidence that, after seven years of relating to the village only insofar as it served her real estate ambitions, Ms. Property Value next door landed on *this* week to take a stand against the Gallegos drug family. Two *vatos* from the compound were unusually agitated, driving erratically up and down our dirt road in a sedan with Arizona plates, pulling onto busy 76 and then bizarrely freezing in the middle of the road. They also parked at the bridge. I don't know what they were doing in there — freaking out, shooting up, plotting to fill the sudden hole in marketing — but the developer charged the sedan, shook a velour fist, and shrieked epithets.

I was always flattered that people mistook me for her, a woman fifteen years my junior. But on this day I was not particularly jazzed by the synchronicity of body type and hair color. I left the house a few minutes after her outburst, and lying in wait at the place where the dirt road meets 76, they came after me — revving their engine, tailing my bumper, and looking mean. After two miles of this my blood was running like *acequia* water: thin. I pulled over at Earl's vegetable stand and started loading corn, squash, and beans into a paper bag like I was cooking for Chimayó's Fiesta de Santiago y Santa Ana. They drove by all low 'n slow, glaring at my face, then shoulders breasts hips legs *huaraches*, and back to my face again.

That's how it went. I flagged down Officer Quiñones about a mile from Earl's. He was our patrol-man-from-heaven. San Antonio-born, dedicated, sharp — and willing to break role when the situation allowed. There was that time a *tecato* lifted a pair of earrings out of a friend's car in my driveway. I have a stuffed animal tacked up on the carport eave, and as the other officer was checking for fingerprints, Quiñones raised his flashlight to the bear's face and asked, "Did you see anything?" My friend and I shrieked in hilarity. Now, in seriousness, Quiñones instructed me to drive to head-quarters and report the incident. Then he cocked his head as if to share a casual tidbit.

"I don't know why someone hasn't picked up that Gallegos guy," he mused. "I'm pretty sure we have a warrant out for him." It was a soothing comment. But also odd, as if some important detail were missing.

"Hey, if *I* can find him," I thought, "why can't *YOU?!*"

September 29. State Police Captain Quintin McShan is quick to point out that interdiction makes little-to-no dent in the scope and scale of the drug trade, while it puts officers' lives at risk.[63] Read: it's not worth the effort. But what happened in Chimayó on September 29, 1999 was historic.

Six a.m. The church bells at Holy Family pealed across the valley. Linda Pedro awoke to the roughness of male voices too close to her bedroom window whisper-shouting, "GET DOWN!", then helicopter pinions wracking the pre-dawn air. Quiñones describes the morning as the most satisfying of his career. Even Joaquin, when he heard of the drug bust, exhibited an edge of glee.

A squadron of police cars the length of ten cow pastures cruised into the village. Three helicopters hovered and whizzed like dragonflies, and an army of 150 officers — local, state, DEA, and FBI — descended. Five cars glided over the pebbles to Josefa Gallegos' pink stucco house like a submarine in dark water. Agents in black jackets burst in shouting, "DON'T MOVE!" Officers charged Fat José's trailer with guns pointed. "POLICE!" They invaded the three mobile homes at the Barela compound, and seven miles down the road, a caravan surrounded Daniel Franco's single-wide across from Orlie's gas station in Santa Cruz.

Quiñones was assigned to Josefa Gallegos' *tiendita*, which was fine with him as he and Officer David Martinez had spent many an hour sitting across from there in the parking lot at Montoya's hardware, watching the action. Or stopping the action with their watching. "The store is open," they'd report over the police radio. "The store is closed." Once one of the Gallegos brothers came out of the pink stucco and slammed the gate shut right in front of them. "Hey! Is the candy store open today?" shouted Martinez. Another time one of them chided Quiñones for harassing him. "You should be happy I'm here," he called back. "This is a baaa-ad neighborhood. I'm *protecting* you!"

Right before he went in, Quiñones told the FBI agent he was partnered with, "You better wear your gloves." "Naaa-aah," the guy dismissed the warning — and they kicked open the door to Brain Gallegos' shed behind the main house. The FBI man grabbed the suspect from his cot and threw him to the floor. Then he saw it. "Oh my *GA-AWD!!*" Brian's forearms were pricked and punctured beyond recognition, bleeding pussing eaten out rotten gorey. The agent snapped back like a mechanical bull. He'd never in all his days seen open sores so bad. But what would you expect?

Río Arriba was making a sweep of the competition in the other drug categories, why not First Prize "Worst Ever Puncture Holes"?

Quiñones had on leather gloves. He pulled Brian up by the shoulders, clapped on handcuffs, and pushed him into the morning darkness.[64]

As the sun lifted over the Sangre de Cristos on September 29, the top three drug families of Chimayó, plus a fourth group of Mexican nationals, marched single-file into the National Guard Armory in Española for booking. In all there were thirty-one people — Brian, Josefa, Fat José, Felix Barela, Teddy Barela, Jesús Martinez, "Tejano" Santana Mendoza — with another three yet to be caught. There was a shit-load of confiscated paraphernalia too. Black Tar BBs. Black Tar in balloons. Black Tar in plastic bags. Cocaine rolled up in paper bindles like little flags. Cocaine in bags. Marijuana. Valium. Medical syringes. Smoking pipes. Tourniquets. Loaded .38-caliber semi-automatic pistols.

David Martinez had not been on duty the morning of September 29. It was his day off. Yet everyone

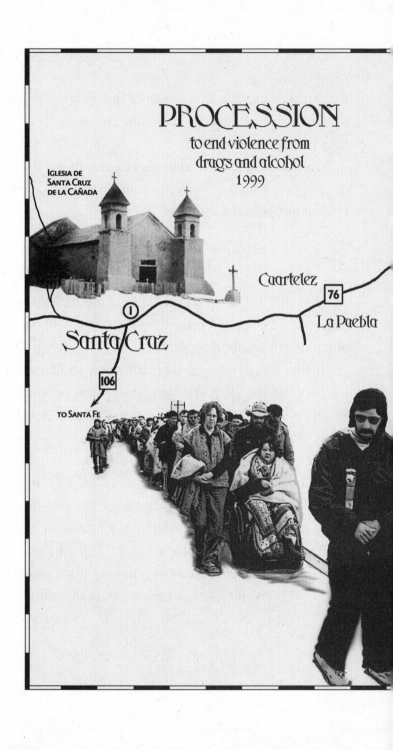

PROCESSION
to end violence from
drugs and alcohol
1999

IGLESIA DE
SANTA CRUZ
DE LA CAÑADA

Cuartelez
**76**
La Puebla

**1**
Santa Cruz

**106**

TO SANTA FE

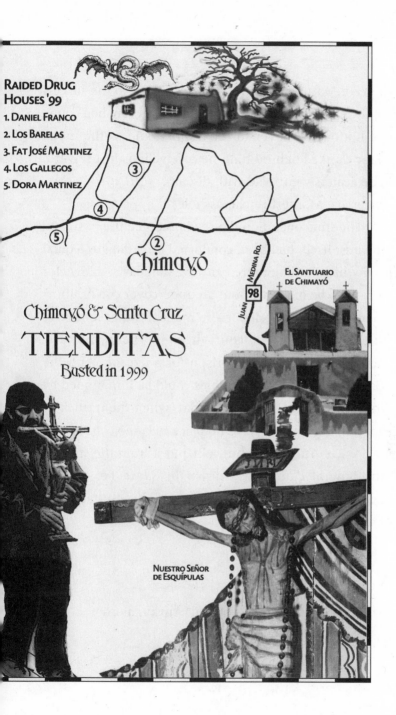

**RAIDED DRUG HOUSES '99**

1. DANIEL FRANCO
2. LOS BARELAS
3. FAT JOSÉ MARTINEZ
4. LOS GALLEGOS
5. DORA MARTINEZ

③

④

⑤

② Chimayó

JUAN MEDINA RD.

98

EL SANTUARIO DE CHIMAYÓ

Chimayó & Santa Cruz

TIENDITAS

Busted in 1999

NUESTRO SEÑOR DE ESQUÍPULAS

agreed: Martinez's work had been crucial to the success of the effort. When he heard that the big day had come, he hotfooted it over to the armory, and as the metal door clanked behind him, he received his just reward. The dealers went wild with disdain. *"¡CHINGÓN!"* they sneered. "Motherffffuckerasshole!"[65]

The sting operation that had preceded the bust, and the bust itself, had been conducted according to federal law which, unlike more exacting state laws, allows for arrests to be made without an undercover cop or informant witnessing a sale. It also mandates that sentences last the full time the court dictates. The upshot: the defendants could go to prison for a decade. And the Gallegos and Barela properties could be impounded by the government and sold so that, when the traffickers got out, they would have no place to land.

As US Attorney John Kelly put it from the steps of the federal courthouse down in Santa Fe, "We've taken a very significant bite out of the well-established narcotics distribution."[66]

The supply line. Always poised. Always alert.

1999: Afghanistan. Sure enough, ten years after the US had sided with the Taliban to beat out the Soviets, Taliban poppy fields were swelling across 225,000 acres and heroin labs speckled the Afghan-Pakistan border like beads from a broken rosary.[67] The country was turning out 4,000 tons a year. Read: 70 percent of the world's illicit opiates.[68]

Then, in July 2000, the right hand suddenly got the better of things. The US government pressed $3.2 million on the Taliban to launch a United Nations-sponsored ban on poppy production. Within months the harvest plummeted to eighty-one tons, an amount that was grown almost entirely by the forces that had battled against the US during the Soviet invasion and one year later, in a post-September 11 turnabout, would become our allies: the Northern Alliance.[69] But most of Afghanistan's crop was sold to non-American users in Iraq, Iran, Pakistan, and Europe. Only 20 percent of the heroin seized in US cities in the late 1990s was Afghani; the other three-quarters was coming from Mexico and Colombia.[70]

*Como siempre*, Mexico.

But Colombia? It seemed an unlikely source. Opium cultivation had been unknown in the Andes region — until, as National Police General José Serrano tells it, "(In 1991 and '92) we found that more than 100 Afghans and Pakistanis had applied for tourist visas (in) Quito, Ecuador, and La Paz, Bolivia, and we believe they were the ones who taught the Colombians how to cultivate heroin."[71] To be sure, Colombia had been involved in the cocaine trade since the 1970s. Using small planes to transport first Bolivian- and Peruvian-grown, then locally grown narcotics to the US, dealers in the cities of Medellín and Cali had built themselves a world-class industry. In the 1990s they diversified and, by 2000, were using their established cocaine channels to supply heroin to the US market.[72] *Chiva*, it turned out, was more compact, easier to slip over borders, and more profitable — and Colombia was a lot closer to American dollars than Afghanistan or Southeast Asia.

As you might guess, the US government was not sitting idly by through all of this. No. It was madly donating military technology to those traffickers that pledged themselves to US-conceived political goals in the region. The tale here is similar to the story we already know of government involvement in the drug business during the Cold War. We meet again the US's irrepressible drive to assert its command over resources beyond its shores, its propensity to invent absolute enemies whose existence fuels the absoluteness of the mission. In the late 1980s, when communism as a viable threat to national security was crashing, US President Ronald Reagan came up with a new Dragon: drugs. For the first time in US history, fighting narcotics production became a military affair, and beyond the CIA, DEA, and Agency for International Development already engaged in the battle, a telling new agency was added: the Department of Defense.

Colombia was in the midst of civil war. The US identified the new enemy in that Latin American country as leftist rebel groups who, initially moved to action by their desire for a more egalitarian society, did indeed foot the bill for their efforts by taxing peasant drug growers. Indigenous tribes and peasants were now considered suspect too — peoples whose claim to land pitted them against corporations seeking oil, coal, and water and whose traditions made them unlikely factory workers or consumers.

But the new enemy in Colombia was *not* the army or the right-wing paramilitary groups, known as the armed-wing-of-the-middle-class, who championed global capitalism — and *also* funded their efforts with money derived from drug production.

A billboard in a left-occupied zone reads: *"PLAN COLOMBIA: LOS GRINGOS PONEN LAS ARMAS, COLOMBIA PONEN LOS MUERTOS"* — "PLAN COLOMBIA: THE UNITED STATES SUPPLIES THE ARMS, COLOMBIA SUPPLIES THE DEAD." Plan Colombia, the US's aid package, is the priciest rendition of the war on drugs in history. Its original outlay in 2000 was $1.3 billion to be distributed to the nations of the Andes region, of a total $7.5 billion to be given by 2005. Its stated intent was to gain control of the country, some 40 percent of which is dominated by leftist guerrilla forces,[73] and to facilitate "nation-building." Nation-building is defined as political and economic stability so that multinational corporations, facilitated by the North American Free Trade Agreement and the proposed Free Trade Area of the Americas, can make use of the region's resources while transitioning a population of land-based peoples into dependency on wages and consumer goods.

For the US government, *drug trafficking is a business endeavor you put up with to your advantage, use to your advantage, or squelch to your advantage.* In this case, US analysts see the business as a source of violence and instability, and so the goal is to squelch it. Eradication and interdiction are the chosen means: fumigate the region's poppy, coca, and marijuana fields and jail the traffickers-of-choice.

And yet, curiously, the bulk of Plan Colombia money does not pay for aerial dusters. Nor for replacement agricultural projects like corn fields. Nor a domestic peace process. No. Eighty percent of Plan Colombia's aid package goes to military training and equipment like A-37 Dragon Fly fighter planes and Black Hawk helicopters — offerings that are used by the army and its right-wing sidekicks to suppress rebel unrest and to nation-build a pro-US regime.[74] To boot, says University of California professor Peter Dale Scott of the Andes region in general, "In the end, the very planes that are sent to keep drugs from coming into this country may be the planes which bring drugs back, as certainly the planes sent to Vietnam repeatedly brought drugs back to the US."[75]

And take note: the chemical herbicide glyphosate, as well as the bio-warfare agent *fusarium oxysporum* used for fumigation are sometimes aimed directly at peasant communities rather than at marijuana, coca, or poppy fields, and these targeted communities typically lie in southern states like Putumayo whose lands are coveted by transnational companies for oil and gas extraction.

In the process, children are burned. Babies are born with deformities. Skin, respiratory ailments, temporary blindness, and cancers have become epidemic,[76] and in response to the poisoning, violence, and government removal projects, two to three million Colombians — the third largest displaced population in the world — have fled to cities and other countries.[77] Many, too, are killed by right-wing troops attempting to "cleanse" them from the area. "People are brought forward and murdered in front of their fellow villagers," reports journalist Marcel Idels. "Sometimes they are shot, sometimes they have their heads bashed in with rocks, and sometimes the paramilitaries utilize hatchets and chainsaws."[78]

Meanwhile the northern region of Colombia, held by right-wing groups, escapes both toxic dusting and removal. And yet, in reality, the north is where the bulk of drug growing takes place.[79] And for all the "This Is Your Brain On Drugs" and the "Just Say No" messages on TV — heroin, cocaine, and marijuana continue to move out along the supply lines. By 2002 Colombia is the source of 80 percent of the world's cocaine[80] and 60 percent of the US's heroin.[81]

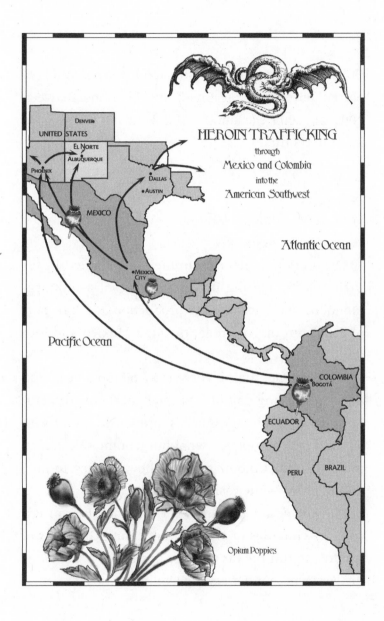

HEROIN TRAFFICKING
through
Mexico and Colombia
into the
American Southwest

Opium Poppies

Colombia White. Bitter-tasting and soluble. Chic. 90 percent pure. Inject me. Smoke me. Snort me. Between 2001 and 2003, the amount of Colombia White shipped into the US triples.[82]

Truth is, you don't always know who the enemy is.

In prison, especially.

Miguel and Gilberto Orejuela are hauled in for their roles in setting up one-mother-of-a-military-monolith to orchestrate the production and transport of drugs out of Colombia, through Mexico and into the US. The year is 1995.

At the time, their income is $7 billion a year, and aside from using half of it to quell local government, business, and military officials' propensity for private jets and beach houses,[83] what burgeoning safe-haven projects inside Colombia might they be using to hide — and grow — the cash?

*¿Dentro de la pinta, quién es el enemigo?* From their country-club digs in prison, Miguel and Gilberto are still free to run the biz without missing a single planting. Or shipment. Or revenge killing. Or investment.

Then — unexpectedly and prematurely — they walk. The year is 2002.

*¿En la sociedad, quién es el enmigo?* President Alvaro Uribe is known for his opposition to the leftist guerrillas who are taxing southern Colombia's coca and poppy growers, as well as his enthusiasm for US-protected oil drilling in the area – and indeed he does give good public outrage at the purported injustice of the release.[84]

But maybe something unseen is afoot. Economic historian Michael Ruppert thinks the Orejuelas are released to make sure Colombia's heroin business will make good in the (as-of-2002) new competition with the poppy producers of Afghanistan, now free to plant again under US occupation.[85] Then in 2004, not contradicting Ruppert's hunch, the US trumps Uribe's urge for a competitive narco-economy. In a round of anti-drug fanfare, the Big Stick to the north demands the extradititon of Gilberto Orejuela for prosecution inside the US.

"Who is the enemy?" It's a good question. But how it plays out is determined by a bigger one: "Who's in control?"

The supply line. The stuff comes up from Colombia through Mexico. The US's southern neighbor has become the main conduit for heroin coming north from the Andes. It has also become a grower in its own right — with opium farms traced to Guerrero, Sinaloa, Durango, Chihuahua, Nayarit, and Oaxaca and trafficking routes from Sinaloa, Nayarit, and Michoacán to Sonora,[86] just south of Phoenix.

Heroin definitely comes into the Española valley from Mexico. The link to the Gallegos, Barela, and Martinez *tienditas* was made evident by two breaks in the pre-September 29 investigation.

The first was the discovery of the badly-beaten body of Aurelio Rodriguez Zepeda, a suspected dealer from Nayarit, in the trunk of a car abandoned in an *arroyo*. The car had been registered to Josefa Gallegos the day before. A cell phone bill found in it tied several of the dealers in Chimayó to each other and gave agents phone numbers to use to arrange "buys" that would help document transactions.

The second break occurred at the federal level. Authorities were busy tracking the movement of drugs from Mexico to California, through Phoenix, and on to northern New Mexico. Perhaps he was an undercover cop, perhaps an informant — whoever —

he made arrangements with Nayarit dealer Armando Vibanco Contreras to bring drugs into *el norte*. A few days later the two couriers named in the call were arrested at the Albuquerque airport, just in from Phoenix, their bags stuffed with heroin and cocaine.

The pieces to a complicated puzzle were coming together. Agents were amassing evidence for a pipeline, and indeed the Operation Tar Pit bust that took place in Phoenix seven months after the Chimayó bust, arresting 249 and garnering sixty-four pounds of heroin, brought down the entire Vibanco Contreras organization. It also unveiled the existence of a network reaching from Tepic in Nayarit north — to Phoenix, San Diego, Honolulu, Portland, Denver, Cleveland, Charleston, Pittsburg, and Albuquerque.[87]

Chimayó, it turned out, was not just an end-destination for Black Tar heroin. It was a jump-off point to other markets.

Black Tar/Mexican Mud. Brown, gummy, and cheap. Place a lump in a sawed-off Coke can. Heat with a Bic lighter. Pour into a syringe.

Life in Chimayó was different after the bust. Things changed. Linda Pedro wept with relief: Fat José had been hauled away. The Penitentes filled their *moradas* with chants of gratitude. I realized what an enormous load maintaining my strategic relationships with the dealers had been, and when the burden dissipated, my energy soared. A handmade sign appeared at the post office: "THANK YOU TO GOD."

"You can feel the change in the air," said Bruce Richardson. "It's like this black-tar cloud was lifted from the valley."[88] According to McShan's office records, breaking-and-entering plummeted by 47 percent in the months after the bust.[89] Local and state police, FBI, and DEA had labored long, hard, and with personal danger to themselves. Richardson and the crime prevention group had drafted the first-ever maps of the *tienditas* and then pushed for the crucial inclusion of federal agencies in the effort.

And yet, truly, no one who marched that overcast day in May doubted that, in the realm of the unseen, the Procession to End Violence from Drugs and Alcohol had been the thing to stir the wind.

# VII.

The overdoses continued. In fact, we witnessed a surge after the bust. The reason? Lines of distribution had been cut, and the *tecatos*, desperate for their fixes, got creative: they began to cook up a deadly concoction of cocaine and the prescription opiate Lortab.

A stranger in a pickup truck honked his horn in my driveway. That's how you make your presence known around here: you honk your horn. The man's plaid flannel shirt was buttoned up all wrong, and the bench seat of his Chevy was littered with crushed Bud

Light cans. Where are you from? I asked. He hesitated. Ojo Caliente. It was a village a good twenty-five miles to the north.

The man locked his frantic eyes to mine. "Help me," he pleaded. "I need *chiva*."

I am still horrified at what I did next for I was momentarily filled with the bravado of having beat the dealers out of town. "You know where the Santuario is?" I asked. "Drive out this dirt road. Turn right, then right again at Juan Medina. Go pray for yourself."

Inside the house, on my desk, lay a neon-orange flyer with phone numbers to call to get help. I crumpled into a heap of sobs for my insensitivity.

In October Española Hospital treated nine people for overdoses; two died.[90] The deaths continued into 2000. "Physiologically there's nothing more addictive to the human body than heroin," Española's police chief Wayne Salazar told the *Albuquerque Journal*. "We see (heroin addicts withdrawing) here in jail. It's just traumatic."[91] A Chimayoso named Alfonso Martinez succumbed in January. Over in Chamita Thomas Rodriguez's girlfriend discovered his cold body lying next to a spoon cooker and syringe. Upon returning home from her own rehab, Norman Valdez's wife found him dead of a morphine overdose; he had been in recovery at Amistad. Carlos Martinez died from a mix of heroin, cocaine, and alcohol. Friends dropped Gilbert Trujillo at the Española Hospital ER after they discovered him unconscious in an *arroyo*. There were women too: Cathy Chacón passed out on a couch at the Santa Clara Apartments. Lisa Tafoya died up the mountain in Chamisal.

Of the seven guys he used to shoot up with, Joaquin offered, he was the only one still alive.

Something else happened. It was as if invisible fingers had been busily drumming at the edge of the action and then, the moment the dealers were cleared out, they sprung. Here we were barely disentangling ourselves from the clench the dealers had had on us. Before September 29 precious few in the village had even been able to form words around the machinations behind the robberies. Few had dared to name the dealers outloud or even speak the word *chiva*.

And then — lo and behold, big and bold — New Mexico Governor Gary Johnson showed his hand: he wanted to *legalize* heroin, cocaine, and marijuana.

His thinking was based on the growing failure of the effort to suppress drug abuse by interdiction abroad, intercepting shipments at the borders, and arrests of dealers and users at home. In 1972, the federal anti-drug budget was $101 million; in 1980 it was roughly $1 billion; by 2004 the amount had shot up to $30 billion,[92] with the fifty states spending that much again.[93] And these expenditures only covered the enforcement of drug laws; they did not include the fiscal impact of criminalization on the public health and criminal justice systems. Still, with all the outlay of monies, drugs did not dry up in the US. As retired San Jose police chief Joseph McNamara reported at a 1999 tribunal on narcotics, they became cheaper, purer, and more plentiful.[94] Law enforcement itself was admitting that the Saint-Michael-versus-the-Dragon approach was failing. "As a nation we now have nearly half a million people behind bars on drug charges, more than the total prison population in all of Western Europe," wrote Johnson in a *New York Times* editorial.[95] Indeed, by 2001 the proportion of the US prison population who were drug offenders had reached 55 percent.[96]

In New Mexico, 81 percent of the $159.7 million the state spent on corrections went to problems stemming from drugs and alcohol abuse.[97] In Río Arriba county, 75 percent of arrestees tested positive for drugs[98] — with 70 percent of men on opiates[99] — and according to a public defender serving Río Arriba, 90 percent of criminal cases in the county were related to chemical dependency.[100]

Like his counterparts in the left and liberal wing of the anti-drug effort, our Republican governor linked drug abuse with poverty. "The burden of this explosion in incarceration," he wrote, "falls disproportionately on black and Latino communities."[101] While African Americans make up only 12.2 percent of the population, they comprise 59 percent of those doing time for drug offenses.[102] A similar link was being made in *el norte*. We were #1 in drug overdose deaths, and according to the 2003 Río Arriba Comprehensive Community Health Profile, 39 percent of the county's Hispano residents had not completed high school,[103] while 22.5 percent lived in poverty.[104] Forty percent lacked health insurance.[105]

I drove up to Taos to see some films with a couple of friends. The subject matter was mountains, and since poppy and coca are often grown in mountain regions, the films to be shown that afternoon would be about drugs. Governor Johnson was scheduled to talk. He was OK, I guess. There was something odd about him: here the guy was blowing the lid off the conversation by advocating legalization — and yet his arm had to be yanked and twisted to get any money for rehab. And he kept building bigger prisons.

In Taos, the *films* were the thing.

The drug war in Latin America was not going well. Jarring images bled into each other the way the realities of unjust political situations always do. Military boots. AK-47s. Innocent citizens plucked off city streets and caged in wooden crates. A line-up of indigenous men pressed into servitude at coca farms in Bolivia, forced to spout cheers for the day's productivity like a Wal-Mart employee pep rally. Black Hawk helicopters spewing poison. Dead chickens. Babies with their brains oozing outside their heads. Singed crops — and afterward, the locals frantically replanting them like ants repairing their hills. With the onslaught of cheap agricultural products made possible by free trade agreements, people must grow drug crops just to survive.

My friend Felicia Trujillo was vehement. An athlete and traditional healer, drug politics was not her usual terrain of concern. "I was shocked that this is allowed to continue!" she howled. "And the price? Billions. It all just enforces how the 'civilized' still treat indigenous people as half-human. Locals having to work as troops slashing and burning the fields that could be used to produce food. Everything poisoned. And sure, there are bad drug people. But most of them are involved just so they can eat. The drug war isn't stopping *anything!*"[106]

As we pulled away in the Jeep, legalization activist Lisa Law waved us over. She had a video camera. "What did you think of the films?" she asked. "God. After seeing all that," I responded into the lens, "how could you *not* be in favor of legalization?"

My thinking is actually more convoluted. Yes, both at home and abroad the drug war is a failure. Legalization would put a halt to the violence perpetrated by dueling cartels, and for those imprisoned in Bolivian farms or trapped in wooden cages in Bogotá, it would bring freedom. Legalization would give addicts a chance to recover or get high or go down the tubes — whatever — without hurting anyone else, and harm reduction programs like needle exchanges would cut down on the spread of diseases like HIV and hepatitis.

But as a member of a community engulfed in the desperation perpetrated by drug dealing, I have a confession: dragging the Gallegoses, Barelas, and Martinezes out of town came not one moment, and one death, too soon. When an independent radio producer called to get a sound bite of civil-liberties outrage at the government's confiscation of their properties, I surprised her — and myself — when I blurted out: "We *want* them to lose their houses! Good Lord, we just got rid of them. We don't want them coming *back!*"

A rarely mentioned detail of the legalization endeavor is that it would only transfer the massive profits garnered from illegal cartels to multinational pharmaceuticals — and violence perpetrated by corporations is as vicious as violence by drug lords, while slavery by economic necessity is as tyrannical as slavery at gunpoint. It is within the realm of possibility too that legalization would *increase* addiction. It happened in China when, in the wake of legalization laws forced by the British, opium addicts grew to 27 percent of the adult male population. It happened in the US with legal opiates when the rate of addiction reached twice what it is today.[107] Look at alcoholism after Prohibition.

And has anyone worked out a blueprint for the transition from cartel to pharmaceutical control? The governments of several countries in the world today are indistinguishable from the business of trafficking, and in many the traffickers are as high-tech heavily armed as a national military — or they *are* a national military.

Two things are for sure. One: the relentless expansion of profit-making endeavors through history we call empire has forged the colossal organization of mass society, everywhere engendering fragmentation of institutions one from the other, fragmentation of sectors of society, fragmentation of self interest, and fragmentation of how people perceive self interest. Complex predicaments result — like the interweaving of global trafficking with personal suffering and addiction — presenting contradictions for which no single solution can be complete.

Two: beyond the complexity of the pro's and con's of legalization lies a bottom line as bold as a felt-tipped slash. Humans have always sought means to attain altered states of consciousness. The glitch: people displaced to mass society typically seek fulfillment outside the ceremonial container that has traditionally guided the experience and given it meaning. And that container cracks into one more lost shard with each season that we do not return to the sustainable ways of farming, gathering, hunting, and fishing or understand our existence in spiritual terms.

Just as Governor Johnson became the highest ranking elected official in the country pushing for legalization, so the shit hit the fan. Liberal groups around the country were thrilled with this unexpected shot in the arm. According to his office down in the capital, public reaction was running "97 to 3" in favor of the governor's position.[108] Former US Secretary of State George Schultz sent a surprise endorsement, and Libertarians in New Mexico filed with the Federal Election Commission to draft Johnson for president. (He declined.) A bill he endorsed to give legal go-ahead for public servants to administer the opiate overdose-blocking drug naloxone passed the Senate unanimously — and yet, at the same time, Johnson suspected that his future as an elected official could be washed up.

He was right. Law enforcement, community activists, and parents throughout New Mexico were enraged. At a gathering at the Albuquerque Police Academy, Sandoval county sheriff Ray Rivera called for Johnson's resignation. President Clinton's drug secretary Barry McCaffrey blasted him as a "political oddity."[109] Parents at De Vargas Middle School in Santa Fe staged a protest to bar the governor from coming on campus. Santa Fe city councilor Peso Chavez drafted a resolution to denounce the stance, calling it "irresponsible, thoughtless, and careless."[110]

Officer Quiñones just rolled his eyes.

In the midst of all the gusts and eddies, something else was riding the wind. Something good. The community was organizing.

With the news of New Mexico's status as the #1 overdose state in the nation, proposals for federal funds aimed at prevention and treatment were suddenly leaping from ground to figure from the piles of competing proposals. New Mexico's long-time senator, Pete Domenici, secured a Department of Justice grant of $750,000 for Río Arriba to provide after-school alternatives to substance abuse and criminal activity. He also got money to boost the Boys and Girls Club in the region and facilitate the continuation of the law-enforcement effort.

After initially vetoing a drug treatment bill, Governor Gary Johnson was convinced to give the go-ahead to a $1 million pilot project. The NM Department of Health chose an Arizona company to set up the area's first outpatient treatment center focused specifically on heroin abuse, and Amity, Inc. renamed itself Amistad de Nuevo México for its launch into Spanish-speaking country. An eight-year outlay of money by the Department of Health was also launched. Plus, local and national foundations began to take an unprecedented interest in *el norte*.

Some of the Española valley's already existing programs were beneficiaries of this focus. Hoy Recovery Program was one of them. A *norteño* named Abe Torres had started Hoy thirty years before when he shuttled alcoholics the hour-and-a-half across the mountains to

Alcoholics Anonymous meetings in Las Vegas. It now had a residential and outpatient facility on Paseo de Oñate. With grants from foundations, the state, and federal agencies Hoy was able, as director Ben Tafoya put it, to "diversify"[111] — expanding to administer DWI programs for courts and setting up a much-needed referral service to residential treatment.

Hands Across Cultures had been founded in 1995 by Harry Montoya. As a mental health counselor frustrated by the various economic and political roadblocks to providing adequate treatment, Montoya had a vision. He wanted to offer the community services that would help people *not start* using drugs and alcohol in the first place. By 1999 Hands Across Cultures had produced several award-winning educational videos including *"La Cultura Cura"* and *"Jornada del Muerto,"* both of which depict the impact of drug addiction on *norteños* and present traditional culture as the means for overcoming it. After the drug bust, Hands Across Cultures garnered grants to build a teen center; offer classes on drug use, violence, and domestic abuse in Española; open a Boys and Girls Club next to the Chimayó elementary school; and foster a mentoring program.

Another institution to receive monies was the Río Grande Treatment Center, which was funded for increased services at its residential clinic in the village of Embudo. And Ayudantes, offering counseling and methadone to heroin addicts since 1983, signed contracts with the state to continue its work with the added attention of research studies to gauge effectiveness. The tiny Una Ala clinic, on the old highway to Los Alamos, began to work in conjunction with Hoy, supplementing methadone treatment with support services.

It was a time for those with track records to keep on keepin' on. It was also a time for trailblazers.

A new effort that got started was the Black Tar Heroin Initiative. Its goal was to rally community leaders to respond to what police, health professionals, and *tecatos* alike were insisting was the source of the problem: cheap heroin coming up from Mexico. The group brought together people who normally did not meet with one another — folks from Eight Northern Indian Pueblo Council, Santa Fe and Río Arriba counties, the Department of Health, non-profits like Hands Across Cultures, Río Arriba Family Care Network, and Santa Fe Community Partnership — "building coalitions on the community level."[112] They set up a system for at-risk families to receive government services to deflate stresses, like violence or lack of medical care and housing, that contribute to drug abuse.

It was also a time for faith. Many of the people in the Black Tar Heroin group were the religious leaders who had marched in Linda Pedro's procession. "When the Hermanos walked," reported one brother from a *morada* in the north, "we had an experience of bringing communities together, with the Hermandad participating for the first time, and big changes started to happen."[113]

One change was something previously unheard-of in the faith community. A Pentecostal minister, two Roman Catholic priests, a Presbyterian minister, and several Hermanos traveled together to a week-long training given by the Pacific Institute for Community Organizing of California. PICO's teachings were based on the philosophy of liberation theology. To attend to people's souls while ignoring their needs for food, shelter, and human dignity, the philosophy stated, is nothing short of blasphemy. One of its earliest proponents, the Peruvian Gustavo Gutiérrez, challenged the Catholic Church to redefine the ministry as a project of helping people rise up against injustice. "Only through concrete acts of love and solidarity," he submitted in *A Theology of Liberation*, "can we effectively realize our encounter with the poor and the exploited and, through them, with Jesus Christ."[114]

After this first PICO training, and several subsequent ones, the faith-based community of northern New Mexico was eager to take up the ministry of liberation theology.

The county had been active since the mid-1990s. As then-chairman of the county commission Alfredo Montoya describes it, services were "at each other's necks for the same dollars" and so the commission launched an effort to "save our families from being overwhelmed by substance abuse." They formed the Río Arriba Family Care Network to gather all the disparate efforts.

"One of the first things is we had to look at ourselves," explains Montoya. "For a person to recover, the first step you have to take is admit you're in a jam. So we said, 'This is going to be embarrassing because we're going to have to come out.' And that's what started this whole thing about our county leading the state and the state leading the nation. We publicly said we have a problem; we called it an epidemic. We sought the help of Senator Domenici to have a public hearing and a townhall meeting to see if we couldn't get resources from outside." The commission hired an Anglo named Lauren Reichelt who, as Montoya tells it, "had worked her way through the ranks and demonstrated she was able to make the contacts that we needed and still be accepted by our service providers as an ally."[115]

Reichelt had come face-to-face with the effects of heroin abuse while building a neighborhood playground in 1993. There she met Annette Valario — Annette's daughter was the girl who had been murdered by an addict stealing her diabetes syringes — and they named the playground for her, Venessa's Hideaway. By 1994 the county had hired Reichelt as a community organizer, and soon she was heading up the Family Care Network. She immediately determined that, fiscally speaking, the county could not build a viable health care system until its rampant substance abuse problem was contained.

"When the issue blew up in the press in '97," she explains now, "it was phrased as a 'Mexican Black Tar Heroin' issue. First of all, it's not a Mexican problem and shouldn't be used to beat up on immigrants; it's our problem. Second, the use of the word 'Black' has the unfortunate side effect of suggesting that only people of color use drugs. And last, it's not just a 'heroin' problem. People make use of whatever high is most readily available to them, whether that's valium or cocaine or alcohol. We couldn't solve the problem simply by removing one drug from the streets."

Reichelt got busy. Working with county officials, community activists, educators, players in the recovery field, and families afflicted by violence stemming from substance abuse, the Family Care Network decided to reframe the issue. "What we have here is a public health problem," she says. "We need more treatment options."

The network also emphasized the importance of the health of the community. "The best way you can fight substance abuse over the long run," she explains, "is to stress community infrastructure, meaning both physical infrastructure like treatment and recreation facilities and also networks of people working together to better themselves, what we call 'social capital.'" The county's approach became to listen to people, hold meetings, form coalitions, march, protest at the legislature, write letters — "anything we could do to get people involved with each other."[116]

Meanwhile, Wayne Salazar became the first police chief in the United States to initiate training for law enforcement officials in the use of injectable naloxone, brand-named Narcan. Administered to a person who has overdosed, according to Jeanne Block of the New Mexico Department of Health, the life-saving drug "knocks the heroin off the brain receptors."[117] The New Mexico state police and Española fire department now carry Narcan in a nasal-spray form.

Indeed, it was a time for trailblazers.

It was also a time for sovereignty. In a place with a history of land-based sustainability, the most important political theme must be self-determination; loss of it is the hallmark of colonization.

After the drug arrests in Chimayó, the Department of Justice came shrieking into *el norte* like gang busters.

Literally. They wanted to fund a task force to be based in the US Attorney's office that would publicly tout the "success" of its anti-drug militarism in Latin America, push for tightened immigration laws as an anti-drug strategy — and hand-feed Río Arriba a "suitable" recovery plan, with an emphasis on police assault. Read: make Río Arriba its "poster county" for the drug war.

Lauren Reichelt was invited to attend a meeting in Pojoaque with a representative of Drug Czar Barry McCaffrey's DC office. She had already had some experience with the DOJ. One agent had pressed her to fashion statistics to document that overdose deaths had plummeted after the bust when he knew that they had shot up. Another wanted the county to "appear" to hold meetings for developing local strategy, but insisted DOJ dictate who would preside, how the meetings would be run, and who would be acceptable to attend.

When Reichelt arrived at the meeting, she was shocked. To begin, a lineup of uniformed generals and National Guardsmen festooned with medals reported their extensive service to the nation. Then McCaffrey's people unveiled their purpose: they were going to produce a series of public-relations spots for national TV with New Mexico children complaining that Governor Johnson's stand on legalization was causing their classmates to use drugs.

Reichelt was not head of Río Arriba's health network for nothing. Military medals or not, she piped up that the governor's ideas should be debated on their own merits or lack thereof. She announced that drug abuse in northern New Mexico is a public health problem, not a criminal justice problem, and that the most relevant "assault" we could mount would be treatment — for *norteños*, by *norteños*, with *norteños* in mind.[118]

The final blow to the plan to make the county with the most per-capita drug overdose deaths a DOJ emblem of success came when Alfredo Montoya graciously — for graciousness is a facet of local etiquette — requested a culturally-sensitive plan. Knowing that the county could use financial help from the federal government, he had tried to work with the agency — meeting endlessly, holding hearings, submitting the grants the DOJ proposed he submit. But in the end their insistence that the county mold itself to their image proved too much, and Montoya stood his ground.

The DOJ left.[119]

# VIII.

Joaquin threw the door to his world open to me, and drug-related goings-on in the community flipped from ground to figure. The waiter at our favorite restaurant, it turned out, had just gotten out of the joint for murder. A pungent vinegary smell infused the house of my low-rider neighbor when we popped in to visit, and there were three men on the lam from parole and one jailbreak at the traditional *matachine* dances at the Casanova night club. On the other hand, a woman named Dee Dee heroically expiated her urges in the lap lane each day at the swimming pool. A handsome young dancer from San Juan Pueblo quaked like a dying deer from methadone withdrawal in the Amistad parking lot, and a bone-thin boy announced in group that he had been clean for a month.

I had an idea. An exhibition of art pieces exploring the ins and outs, ups and downs, of heroin addiction. Growing up a mile from the Cleveland Art Museum had given me something of a feel for Western art, with an emphasis on the breakthrough movements since impressionism. I had a memory of a show that spanned from Seurat to Picasso. In the last room, next to Monet's *Water Lilies*, hung a collection of boxes housing an array of images and items, what they called "found objects." The artist was the surrealist Joseph Cornell; his work dubbed Cornell Boxes. The project I was now catching in glimpses was a series of boxes, each revealing some aspect of the heroin experience — shooting up, dealing, drug cars, the impact on the family — each constructed of actual drug paraphernalia. Joaquin was wild for it.

He balanced his metal chair against the porch post at his mother's trailer and began to sketch. He drew an upright rectangular box framed by prison bars, with a bare light bulb inside. He drew a casket with open drawers around the sides, each one displaying the artifacts of an aspect of the experience that ultimately, he wanted to say, leads to death.

I set out to find drug stuff. For Chimayó this may have been an unusual endeavor — people usually tried to get *rid* of drug stuff — but it was not a difficult one. My first syringe was a gift. Ruth from the framing shop on the plaza gave me a 100-unit syringe she had scavanged by the door to Ortega's weaving gallery.

I headed up County Road 87, an *arroyo* that leads to various *tienditas* and makes an easy dump for *tecatos* shooting up as they make their get-away from a buy. I found three orange-capped syringes and one whose needle was bare. Using latex gloves and the mindfulness of a Buddhist, I lifted the three into a plastic bag in my backpack. Once in the kitchen, I placed them in a Tupperware container filled with Clorox straight-up and never ever removed the caps. Being around the syringes, I always felt as if I were navigating a field of upward-pointing daggers. But I kept at the task. Sure, I could have bought a couple of family packs at La

Farmacia. To my artistic mind, though, the paraphernalia needed to be real.

Joaquin got wind of a whole box of used syringes that the San Juan Pueblo dancer wanted to unload. I met him at his job on the floor of the casino. It was like a drug deal. We spoke in metaphor. He made a call. He told me to meet a woman in a beat-up Honda at the Dairy Queen. I hot-footed it over to the DQ. She pushed a plastic video container into my hand and sped away.

These syringes were not only uncapped; each was carefully broken in two, as if to warn prospective needle-sharers of hepatitis contamination. I kept them for a while in deference to the courage of the young dancer who had trusted me to take away his incriminating materials. Finally, in fear, I packed the whole thing up inside a cardboard box so as not to endanger anyone else, and I put it in the trash.

My idea was to collect the paraphernalia by myself. Drug Court required that Joaquin not spend time around persons or tools having to do with substance abuse. But I kept remembering a tourniquet I'd seen on 87; we didn't have a tourniquet. One day the two of us were driving over there, and expediency won over disgression. We parked my mechanic's borrowed Ranchero in the *arroyo*. Joaquin was just bending over with his latex gloves to pick the thing up and I was standing by with the plastic bag open — when the world turned flashing red and yellow. We froze. And there, in all his black polyester glory, stood a New Mexico state police officer.

Joaquin instantaneously sucked every ounce of energy of his being into a miniscule ball in his stomach. I did the opposite. Mustering my new-found confidence from having shared a few beers with Officer Quiñones, I expanded like a balloon.

"Is that your car?" He was running a check on the Ranchero. (Oh God. Please make it that the mechanic is paid up on his plates.)

"What's the problem?"

"You can't park like that."

Precisely at what angle I had positioned the car on a lone country road seemed a minor event in the grand scheme of things. But with a Drug Court attendee in tow and an artifact of drug culture nearly in the bag, flashing lights and a man with a badge could never be minor.

"Of course. Yes. I'll move it."

"What are you doing here?" he asked to my horror.

"Uh. I'm collecting some stuff for an art project."

"What stuff?"

"Uh … You know. Stuff… Found objects to put in sculptures."

"Oh." He seemed momentarily disoriented, and I took the opportunity to reach into my seat-of-the-pants bag of psychology tricks.

"What's your name?" I asked, meeting his gaze with intensity. "How long have you worked here in the valley?" Suddenly I was the 52-year-old, he the 25-year-old; I was the local, he the outsider — all the while Joaquin was shimmering behind me like a sloughed-off snakeskin on a chamisa branch.

A sometimes-fine line, sometimes-bold slash delineates the space between criminality and political action. Case in point: you should have seen Joaquin's eyes illuminate when I told him how, during anti-war demonstrations in the 1960s, we dodged and challenged the Berkeley city cops, Alameda county sheriffs, and National Guard.

According to sociologist Richard Quinney, defini-
tions of criminal behavior are not absolute: they are
based on the values and goals held by the people in
power in a society. What is dubbed "political crime,"
then, is crossover terrain. It consists of violations perpetrated to protest, express beliefs, or alter how things
are — such as treason, espionage, assassination, violations advocating "radical beliefs" via civil disobedience,
destroying property, or demonstrations; and failure to
conform because of religious beliefs, as in fasting.[120]
Sociologist Robert Merton makes the insightful dis-
tinction between "non-conforming" and "aberrant"
actors. To Merton the non-conformer practices dissent
publicly, with an eye to drawing attention to injus-
tices, often laying claim to a higher moral authority
than that which is assumed. The aberrant acts as invis-
ibly as possible, with an eye to personal gain.[121]

Here in northern New Mexico, county manager
Lorenzo Valdez describes the similarities and differ-
ences between the two by talking about history. A
marked change took place in Río Arriba when the US
government moved in on the *mercedes*, he explains. In
the beginning, when *la gente* fought back, they did so
directly — mounting protests within the Court of

Public Land Claims, unionizing, cutting down the new barbed-wire fences, raiding Forest Service encampments. As the opposition became more forceful and the people more desperate, some *norteños* turned to behind-the-scenes acts which, while still expressive of the *¡Ya Basta!* sentiment of protest for collective justice, took on a more chaotic and individualistic shape. The can-do anarchism of a people scattered across the upland desert — truly its strength — deteriorated into self-inflicting outbursts whose purpose was merely to vent. Chicanos stealing from Chicanos. Murders in the villages. Drugs. *La vida loca.* Domestic violence. Suicide.[122] I would never be the one to judge venting; it is crucial for coping with oppression. It's just that venting doesn't often lead to anything beyond itself. At its worst, it hurts innocent people.

I take my cowboy hat off to the academicians who grapple to define the complexities in our midst. But to be truthful, the relationship between crime and politics must be thornier than classroom categories suggest. If you are living in a land-based culture that is genuinely communal, let's face it: you would have no reason to rob your neighbor. Maybe you'd only take mind-altering substances for ceremonial or socially-beneficial purposes. But if you reside in a mass society whose inherent inequities persist through the power wielded by those deriving the most, you might organize a movement to challenge those inequities. Or you might just go lift what you need. And in frustration or despair you might want to mess up your mind.

To make things more complicated, it could be that the powers-that-be *want* you to mess up your mind. During the 1970s, the FBI mounted counterintelligence infiltrations and raids to wipe out the political organizing of groups like the Black Panther Party, the American Indian Movement, and *La Raza Unida*.[123] All the while, according to journalist Gary Webb, CIA operatives actively participated in the delivery of Colombian cocaine into black neighborhoods in Los Angeles — and took in millions in sales to run their covert war in Nicaragua.[124]

Peter Dale Scott describes the convolutions of this set-up, specifically the resulting demise of radical politics in South Central Los Angeles. "The Black Panthers were essentially destroyed," he says. "Most of them were either in jail or out of the country. Or dead. And what did you have in their place? You had drug dealers. And it turned out that the FBI was not going to mount anything like the campaign against the drug dealers that it had mounted against the Black Panther Party."[125]

The sudden infusion of a drug culture that previously had existed only as a facet of the community had major repercussions. To begin, doing drugs was a draw. The drug business was a draw, and drug culture was a draw. Why not? They brought mental relief in a no-way-out situation. They brought money to poverty, and they brought a style, an identity, a sense of potency to folks stripped of self-esteem. But drugs also crashed through the ghettos, *barrios*, and poor rural communities like a toxic tsunami — importing narcissism, jealousy, terror, violence, illness, and epidemics of death. For many the arrival of the drug world into America's disaffected communities was another form of colonization, putting the final stranglehold on whatever community ties to land, community, and family were still gasping for breath.

As Antionette Tellez-Humble from the New Mexico Drug Policy Alliance tells it:

> Once people of color get past talking about our rage and our sadness at the destruction of people we love, we begin to unravel the preponderance of drug abuse among us. "We've

been oppressed so long," we realize, "and this is one more way they're getting us and one more way they're making it our fault." We begin to see the history of how drugs got to us in the first place, who introduced them, what purpose they had. Have you ever wondered why African Americans are incarcerated at such a monstrously higher rate for drug use than anyone else? Sure, racial profiling and a biased judicial system have something to do with it. But did you know? During plantation days, the owners *fed the slaves cocaine* so they'd work harder and faster. And who brought the stuff into South Central LA in the 1980s? Who is handing it out in Baghdad as we speak?[126]

Pancho Villa was your consummate bad-boy bandit.

Joaquin dug Villa.

According to biographer Ramón Puente, before the Mexican revolution Villa alternated between episodes of thievery and stretches in which he led a quiet life. Between 1901 and 1910 he is known to have murdered at least four people — three ranchers and a snitch — and raided several of the rich *haciendas* that were luxuriating on what had once been the people's common lands.[127] When he allied himself with Francisco Madero to fight the revolution, Villa showed himself to be a creative military strategist — but he also flagrantly aimed the barrel of a gun at his mentor. Whether he was charging around taking on cattle ranchers, working a regular job, or commanding his troops, one thing is for sure: Villa felt wronged by society — and he was given to irrational outbursts of anger.[128] Politics? Crime? Or political banditry? American journalist John Reed called Pancho Villa "the Mexican Robin Hood."[129] Others have simply called him a murderer.[130]

In 1920 the first coherent government to arise out of the revolution offered Villa a somewhat ironic gift: a 163,000-acre *hacienda* in Chihuahua. He gathered up his children and moved in — never saying another word about land reform for the peasants he had supposedly been representing during the fighting years.

Emiliano Zapata, on the other hand, was a political warrior.

I preferred Zapata.

He had been born to a village that had one basic mission: to retrieve the land that in 1607 had been stolen by a neighboring *hacienda* so that the people could continue their land-based tradition. As historian Enrique Krauze puts it, Zapata's homeland was never Mexico; it was the village of Anenecuilo. "Zapata not only knew the whole history of that small universe. He was its embodiment. Everything else was abstract, alien."[131] Using today's language, Zapata's politics could be described as *puro* bioregional/*puro* sovereignty-rights. The Program of Ayala that he fought to achieve delineated a Mexico made up of independent villages, each equal and living in respectful relationship to the others.

Pancho Villa and Emiliano Zapata rode into Mexico City on the famed day — 6 December 1914 — when the Convention of Aguascalientes took the capital to hash out a post-revolution government. A shorthand transcript of their dialog is revealing to the discussion of crime and politics. Villa referred to "bits of land (the people) want" — as if land reform were a side issue; Zapata spoke of "*the* land" — as if it were the reason the revolution had been fought. A jovial Villa placed himself in the Presidential Chair next to a Zapata whose visible discomfort echoed the wariness of his peasant troops in the big city. An eyewitness to the moment remembered: "Villa sat in the chair as a joke, while Emiliano stood to one side, and he said to

Emiliano, 'Now it's your turn.' Emiliano said, 'I didn't fight for that, I fought to get the lands back.'"[132]

As Krauze puts it, "One fought for the sake of the fight, the other for the Program of Ayala."[133]

I threw open the door to my world. Making art seemed a dynamic way to rearrange the energies of whatever wounded dragons were still rattling about inside Joaquin. Making politics could possibly re-channel his urge to fight-for-the-sake-of-fighting. Who knew? Maybe he would become interested in the effort to retrieve northern New Mexico's stolen *mercedes*? One thing I did know: political action requires the same daring that robbing Bank of America or dashing from the Mexican *Eme* require — but can lead to more constructive results. Or, at least, to a more constructive sense of meaning.

I gave Joaquin a copy of *The Wretched of the Earth*. Writing in the 1960s, Martinique psychiatrist Frantz Fanon had been among the first to apply the conceptual skills of a dominant-society education to the experience of colonial oppression. It was the first time

Joaquin had ever seen his own experience in print, and the "oohs," "aaahs," and *"mierdas"* that burst from the sofa were boisterous. Lives dedicated to crime or to political action spring from the same predicament of injustice, we reasoned. They share the same rebellious spirit, we said. They can even lead to the same punishment, we agreed. But they are very different in their goals. We were having a good time.

The complexity involved in achieving a non-criminal life was revealed to me on the morning of September 11, 2001. As we clutched each other before the TV set while the second tower crashed before our eyes, I alternated between gasps of horror for the people inside and realizations of the political profundity of the event. Joaquin said nothing. Essentially, he went blank and never spoke of 9/11 again. I began to consider that his psyche might not have the capacity to handle things that lay outside its immediate struggles.

Maybe, in his lifetime, he would only ever be a bad-boy bandit.

# IX.

The wind in Drug Court was like deadweight. Joaquin went through the motions, calling in each Saturday morning to see if his designated color had come up for random drug testing, checking off the required number of group therapy meetings each week, appearing in court. He had this uncanny ability to glide. No ups. No downs. Just all *suavecito*.

Then, without warning, he'd crack.

One November day he was leaning over the hood of the '84 Nova he was reconstructing. He was thinking well about his prospects for a job at the substance abuse clinic in Alcalde, and he was industriously gathering dowels for his prison-cell Cornell Box. The next day he went all screwy, uncharacteristically festooning himself with fake turquoise jewelry, three garish rings and a brooch askew on his lapel the way a mental patient's personality is askew. He asked me to drive him to his sister's house. It was so cold that the cab of the Jeep never did heat up, and the whole way he wouldn't talk. Then, as we rounded the curve to Loretta's he got agitated, suddenly commanding me not to stop, to drive to the Amigo gas station by Wal-Mart instead. Over there, under an umbrella of fluorescence and microwave, Joaquin slammed the door behind him and shuffled like a wind-up toy toward the convenience store. The next evening, as I was holding him tight on the couch, he confided that he had twenty-four hours to decide if he would engage in a ... *movida*. I knew the term from my work in politics. It doesn't translate well, but you could say it means a "strategic action" — for good or for bad.

That night, for good or for bad, I rolled around the sheets like a neurotic taco, my mind filled with dastardly prospects. Like someone from Joaquin's past was out to get him. Like that someone was the guy down in 'Burque he needed to see but never would when I was present. Like maybe the county was going to take his house away for unpaid back taxes. Like maybe he was hanging out with those guys at the *tiendita* up the mountain, the one displaying nothing except three orange sodas in a warm cooler and ... a two-way radio at the cash register. Whatever, it seemed that something dark and chaotic and irreversible was about to take place.

By morning I was frantic. I found Joaquin at his mother's trailer, a pile of freshly folded laundry in his arms. I offered to drive him over to his house, but on the way I veered to that half-built adobe barn next to the holding dam. He later confessed he thought I was going to pull a gun. For those who know me the image is dissonant, more so a glimpse into Joaquin's state of mind than into mine. But we should give him some credit: I did pull a willow switch. I swatted his arms through down sleeves, his legs through Wrangler jeans, and I shouted, "What's going on?! You're all *weird!!* TELL ME!!"

While my action was successful at bringing Joaquin back to an awareness that better resembled consensual reality, it wasn't studied or informed. What I did was pure intuition. I hadn't yet figured out that Joaquin's forays into deviance were flashbacks from times past in prison, times past in the streets, times past (who knows?) up against his father in LA or in the refectory of the Catholic Church. I only got an inkling about Joaquin's psychic condition the second time he had a flashback. That was when we went to the punk café on Aztec Street in Santa Fe. We sat around pleasantly enough sipping *maté* and strumming Mexican folk songs. The next day Joaquin was frantic with terror and jumping like a startled bird at the sight of cars painted white. I asked him to tell me about this unexpected emotional intrusion, and so unfolded the tale of a drug deal gone wrong, a woman with dyed black hair and too-red lipstick, a shootout … and a white Ford Taurus — all at that very coffeehouse on Aztec.

I asked Joaquin to go over precisely what happened and how he felt at each turn of events. He did, and the fright subsided. I knew then that Joaquin was saddled with a blistering case of post-traumatic stress disorder.

PTSD. It rolls over you like a backhoe. It singes your nerves, burrows right into your brain.

If there's trauma to the head like a punch or a fall, it's possible the waves that course through the brain will flow with less oomph, and the numbing that results could open the way for temper tantrums and hostility.[134] Or maybe the side of the cortex that normally processes emotions freezes up, and a person becomes incapable of feeling the anxiety that would normally link actions to an understanding of their consequences.[135] Maybe what happens is the left side and the right no longer work together.

We know this: the original feelings are too much for both psyche and nervous system to handle, and so they get packed into a separate room. A room with a closed door. In the midst of the original trauma maybe the person has lasered in on just one detail — maybe a white car — and a facsimile of that detail in the here and now is all that's needed to fling the door open. And so you get flashbacks. Emotional bleeding. Unbearable intrusions. "Parasites of the mind."[136]

Joaquin got the job in Alcalde, and just as the folks running Drug Court at Amistad had put him in charge of
the young people in their program, so the clinic placed
him in a position of responsibility. Checking in new
clients. Running therapy groups. Teaching guitar.
Conducting field trips. Addicts loved him. He had tattoos. He was tough. He'd been there. And he dressed the
part. On the first day of work, a Lakota counselor pulled
Joaquin aside to pin down what, to land-based people
the world over, provides the baseline for relationship.

"You're not from here."

"Oh yeah, man, I am. My family's from Chimayó.
All the way back."

"I mean, you've been somewhere else. I'm guess-
ing California. Soledad? A long time ago?"

If you have eyes to see, you can read a person's
history of incarceration by his dress. Joaquin wore
pleated men's pants up high above his waist, flat hard
shoes, a white undershirt tight over his muscles, and
for special occasions a shirt festooned with Chinese
dragons — top buttons fastened, bottom buttons open.
In cold weather he donned a black overcoat that lent
him that certain gangster look. He had Soledad/early
'70s written all over him.

One February night when the stars looked like icicles, Joaquin put on his East LA suit and skinny silver tie, and we drove to Santa Fe to give a lecture about heroin to a group of archetypal psychologists. As I angled the Jeep into an upscale parking spot by the upscale restaurant where we would make our presentation, Joaquin said something I think is relevant across the US. "The #1 place to pick up *chiva* in this city is a block from here."

Sitting atop stools, our backs against a *piñon* fire, we faced a rapt audience most of whom had never been so close to a man with a dragon etched over the track marks on his forearm. We focused on the mythical beast as the symbol of heroin. In China, where opium production began, Dragon represents the life breath. It is stealthy like a spring breeze, sensual like a summer storm, as treacherous as a hurricane — and sacred. Read: Dragon is a creature you *want* to know. But in the West, where a philosophy of rigid duality has evolved, the very qualities of wildness and freedom encapsulated by the Dragon have come to be feared and denigrated. The result is a battle: between human and nature, intellect and feeling, refined and gross, righteous and enemy — and in the world of illicit substances, with Archangel Michael brandishing His sword for law and order against His fiery antagonist.

Joaquin was charismatic on stage. He told flamboyant stories, made points about the dangers of addiction, mimicked a drug deal on a toy cell phone, passed around used syringes from the *arroyos* of Chimayó, and explained he'd been clean for six years. I laid the background for these real-life experiences, relating the history and politics of the heroin trade. Afterward, people flocked around to hear one more tale or share a private word.

Joaquin came up with a title for a continued offering of the speech. My job was to raise the seed money, write the brochure, make contacts around the country. His job was to get the brochure printed. Problems arose. For Joaquin each task needed to be approached. Then re-approached. Then re-approached again. As soon as the errors from the last task were remedied, bizarrely, new errors would arise, errors that had not existed before. The spelling of words. The location of commas. The spelling of other words. The location of other commas. The color of the ink. The weight of the paper. The ink. The paper. The bill. The weight of the paper again. The ink again. The bill again. What could have been a four-day job turned into an eight-month ordeal. I'd never seen anything like it.

When the brochure was finally ready, Joaquin left the house with an envelope holding the entire $700 from the grant I had secured. He paid the $200 printing bill — but when he returned, a total of $400 was missing. Around the time we started getting enthusiastic calls to speak in San Francisco, Boulder, and LA, he downed a single pain pill, failed his Saturday morning urine test at Amistad, and on a dime was clanking up the courtroom aisle with chains on his ankles to beg the judge's leniency.

Maybe his father stood him in the living room and, with a leather cow strap, walloped him. Maybe a group of black boys came upon him in the alley, threw him against the sand, and took turns punching. Maybe, when he went crying for help, his father ordered him to ferret out the attackers and beat them up. (Maybe he was pressed into sexual service to a priest.)

And maybe, if these things happened, the boy was small and thin like a willow. Maybe he was eight years old.

# X.

It was something about going to get help. There was help enough around. Amistad was there. I was there. All those people at the clinic in Alcalde. The former police chief of Española was his new parole officer, and he was as kind as Esquípulas and the Santo Niño combined. But, for Joaquin, getting help carried an onus that even he did not understand. Then, it was something about that irrepressible itch to steal. From banks and businesses. From his mother. From our grant to give lectures. The itch was all raw and bleeding from his personal hurt and from social inequities that no one could deny. Too, it was something about the high he could get from rising up out of hell. Mustering the effort. Pumping iron. Strutting up the dirt road with possibility in his veins. And always always, it was something about a beast so dark and scaly, a conflict so evil and unspoken, it could never wriggle its way into the open. Just to ask for help — *"¡Papa, ayúdeme!"* — would unleash it into a fiery tumult beyond his ability to survive.

Joaquin was trapped. He couldn't see his way to getting help. He couldn't make headway on his own. And, his instinct to prevail being as it was, he couldn't just hurl himself into a pine casket.

If the psyche cannot find its way to healing, it searches for another way, *any* way — constructed, reconstructed, deconstructed — to slap bandages across the wounds. The task that Joaquin could never quite get a handle on was to carry his own weight; he simply did not have the inner resources. When the judge said, "It's time for you to find a job," Joaquin wilted, pleading that he didn't need money to live. When at last he was bringing home a paycheck from the substance abuse clinic in Alcalde, he spent it like a child, buying bouquets of flowers instead of food, splurging on fancy shoes instead of fixing the ailing Nova.

I didn't say anything. When the occasional bag of groceries came through the door, I was genuinely pleased. But the original plan to offer support during his getting-back-on-his-feet period was turning into a longer run than my bank account had anticipated. Still, I watched. And I waited.

He took another pain pill. Again, just one — and Joaquin's approaching graduation from Drug Court was abruptly canceled. His social worker proclaimed, "I *knew* his problem was pills, not heroin," and the judge ordered him to the residential treatment program at Embudo for the summer.

Clearly, Joaquin was struggling with post-traumatic stress. His world was a mine field of people and situations whose propensity to reproduce facsimiles of the people and situations that had harmed him in the first place would not quit. He was constantly navigating his way through the resulting panic, and so his psyche took an inventive tack: it channeled all that unbearable stress into a classic rendition of anti-social personality. Indeed, a panorama of Joaquin's life revealed a ceaseless continuum of fuck-you's, a progression of white lies, as well as a spate of out-and-out deceptions. And those crazy car chases from his drug days. (Even his driving today overshot the centerline like a dare to anyone on the road.) Plus, he had little remorse for anything he had ever done.

I disagreed. I didn't think that the problem was either pain pills or heroin. I thought these were sideshows for drawing attention away from the overbearing clashes of energy and emotion his psyche was required to endure.

But then again, my opinion meant nothing. Amistad had so much chaos to manage with all the addicts going through their stresses, they could hardly take the time to approach deeper psychological structures. And to Joaquin I was talking about a *problem*; when he was socked into his anti-social self, he was so identified with his inventions and projections, he didn't think there *was* a problem.

The problem in the Española valley was that, no matter what community effort was mounted, heroin kept right on coming in. Captain McShan's take on the big drug bust of '99 was that it hadn't been worth the risk to the officers' lives. For sure, Chimayó was better off. But word had it that, after a brief period of disorientation, the nerve centers of the business simply migrated west across the Río Grande to Hernandez and north up the mountain to Peñasco. Word had it too that the Española valley was a jump-off point for shipping drugs from Mexico, via Los Angeles and Phoenix, north to Denver and beyond — and so, to the traffickers masterminding the distribution system, passage through northern New Mexico was essential.

Indeed, today's drug business reflects the geopolitical realities of the 21st century. Like a McDonald's hamburger, heroin can be had just about anywhere in the world. Johannesburg. Karachi. The Tohono O'Odham reservation in Arizona. Liverpool. Plano. Kuala Lumpur. Kiev. Chase the Dragon in Dalton. Rabat. Tampa. Adelaide. Dublin. Budapest. Bremen. Helsinki. Dakar. Tachileik. Nairobi. Hong Kong. Belgrade. Vancouver.

US President Clinton's 1998 installation of the CIA-backed Kosovo Liberation Army as a force in the Balkan region opened an unfettered path for smuggling, from

Opium
Poppies

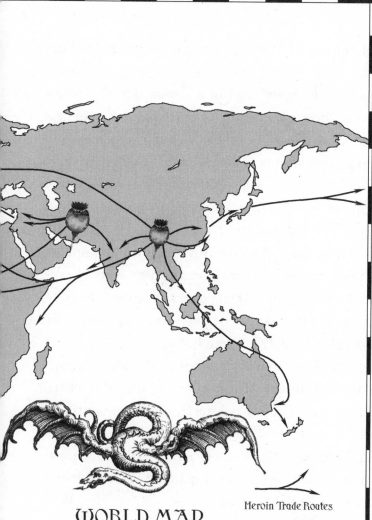

WORLD MAP
exhibiting the
HEROIN TRADE ROUTES
2004

Heroin Trade Routes

Growing Areas

Afghanistan to Western Europe, and the resulting trade route is now moving *chiva* into the Czech Republic, Hungary, and other countries of Eastern Europe. Nigeria is the hub for much of the heroin destined for Africa and Europe. Vietnam is increasingly used as a conduit between SE Asia's Golden Triangle and Australia. Since its entry into the World Trade Organization, China has opened its population not only to cell phones and DVD players, but to its old narcotic standby in a reconstituted form. Colombian chemists are working with Mexican growers to produce Mexican White. Oil pipelines are good venues for smuggling drugs, and Baghdad is now, just since the US occupation, deluged with heroin.

Read: the heroin trade is not a sideshow. Through a daunting history of collusion between traffickers, business and banking institutions, governments and military dating back to the British Empire, the illicit drug trade has come to be essential to the accumulation of capital that fuels the expansion and plunder we call corporate globalization.[137]

Mud. Skag. Smack. *Eroina*. *Hăiluòyiň*. Brown Sugar. *Pasta*. *Hul Gil*. Hell Dust. Pink-Top. A-Bomb. *Carga*. Black Tar. Colombian White. China White. Dragon Rock. *Polvo Blanco*. *Goma*. No. 4. Junk. Crop. Boy. *Heroína*. *La Puta*. *Npwívn*. *Рероɴн*. *Xidu*.

Burma/Singapore: by the turn of the millennium, the most prolific producer of illicit opium in the world. After a military junta grabbed power in 1988 (and against the wishes of the elected party, renamed the country Myanmar), the poppy fields doubled in size.[138] Heroin refineries sprang up in the jungle. In the hills. Anywhere they would fit. By the late 1990s Burma was providing 50 percent of the world's opium[139] and 60 percent of the heroin coming into the United States.[140]

No surprise: in contrast to its post-World War II status as the poorest-of-the-poor, today's Burma oozes with money. Or, shall we say, a select few of its citizens do. Lo Hsing Han stands among them. With his left hand, the heroin kingpin oversees poppy-growing operations in the countryside, a job he openly commandeered for years until an arrest in 1973 that forced him to reconfigure a new public persona. With his right hand, he is a reconfigured persona. Han is the chair of Burma's largest conglomerate, Asia World. His son runs three branches of the corporation in Singapore, while his wife operates an underground banking system from her headquarters at Asia Lite, a subsidiary in Singapore.

The family business? The kind of development activities that have become identified with corporate globalization the world over. A deep-water port in Rangoon, complete with freight handling, storage, and a customs yard. A $207 million industrial park. A $33 million toll highway from the heart of Burma's poppy-growing lands to the Chinese border. A bus line into northern Burma. The ultra-luxurious Trader's Hotel.

"How is it that a company that has a humble beginning trading beans and pulses is suddenly involved in $200 million projects?" asks a US government official who wishes to remain anonymous.[141] A narcotics official answers. "If you're in the dope business," he muses in an interview with journalist Leslie Kean, "these are the types of things that you've got to have to move your product."[142] Dig it: a port, factory space, domestic venues for transport, a high-end resort for visiting "dignitaries."

Another of Burma's development projects is a state-of-the-art cyber-center in Rangoon offering satellite surveillance of all the incoming communications — including telephone calls, faxes, emails, and computer data transmissions — of twenty countries.[143] As Kean and fellow journalist Dennis Bernstein point out, Burma in fact has no foreign enemies. The purpose of such intelligence overkill, they say, is to quell pro-democracy activists[144] in their efforts to challenge a political system based on the subjugation of peasant opium growers, investment of the profits into development aimed at producing more profits, and a military so infamous for its human-rights violations the junta has barred the United Nations from entering.

The money made in drug sales — $1.3 billion a year for Lo Hsing Han alone[145] — disappears into a user-friendly banking system in nearby Singapore, only to re-emerge "clean" and, as the Myanmar-Singapore Ministerial-Level Work Committee has described its task, ready to "forge mutual benefits in investment, trade and economic sectors."[146]

In the swirl of such dealings the source of 50 percent of Burma's economy is unaccounted for.[147] In 1991, for instance, the junta cleaned up $400 million through one bank and then used the money to buy weapons from China—while Burma's foreign exchange reserves registered not one cent of fiscal activity.[148]

Singapore is, of course, an American trading partner of importance: in 2002 US multinationals exported $16.2 billion worth of goods to the island country, and the US enjoyed a $1.4 billion trade surplus.[149] To its credit, the Clinton administration imposed economic sanctions on Burma for its role in bringing heroin to American cities. President George W. Bush followed suit. And yet the US government's enduring right hand remains inflexible, refusing to take a stand on Singapore's role in what has become one of history's most grandiose opium operations.

I traveled to the treatment center in Embudo three times. Once to attend a class on dysfunctional family dynamics — and visit Joaquin. Once to see a play the clients were putting on — and visit Joaquin. Once to participate in a couples counseling session.

It was a beautiful place: an old adobe compound nestled below the road to Taos, among the cottonwoods by the Río Grande. Joaquin's therapist was a *vato* from a village west of Española. In recovery himself, he was brimming with self-disclosure and, as they call it, tough love. It was getting to be autumn, and we sat in a room whose one window opened onto a tantrum of gold leaves.

Joaquin looked like he was on the verge of a tantrum. He was sitting in a cozy chair that nearly enveloped his jumpy body; he had just extended his stay by two weeks for watching TV in a room his category of client was forbidden to enter. The therapist coaxed him to tell me something. He hemmed and hawed. Finally, the therapist said it: Joaquin had revealed that he was intimidated by me.

Oh ... OK. So now what? It was a feeling that needed to be communicated, the therapist skillfully informed me. It wasn't that I needed to mold myself into less than I am. OK, I thought. Joaquin was learning to speak his mind and be accepted without negative repercussion. Yes ... Good.

To my mind, the love between us was strengthened by the exchange: it grew into a golden aura that filled the room and reached outside to the trees and all the way down to the river. The therapist said that, of all the couples he had ever seen, we looked to be the most promising.

When Joaquin walked me to the front doors to say good-bye, he hugged me close. I could feel the familiar curve to his muscles, the warmth of his chest. Then, in guarded earnestness, he whispered into my ear: "They made me say that. I don't feel that way."

And suddenly I was all by myself, out there on the tar of the parking lot amidst a splash of just-peaked yellow leaves. And I was confused.

The drug business. It's confusing.

In 2003 Burma/Southeast Asia lost its position as top heroin producer to the US, and Colombia/Mexico rose to the #1 slot. It is estimated that Colombia was making more than 80 percent of the heroin reaching US streets.[150]

To point the top-dog finger at Colombia has a curious side effect: it makes Americans afraid of Colombia and beefs up public support for the drug war. All the while, Plan Colombia is having its own mobius effect: while boosting the army and paramilitary onslaught against leftist guerrillas, it incites the left to grab more land from land-based peoples to be used for more drug production to fund its efforts, all the while shoring up the narco-business that the right taxes to fund its efforts. And the mobius strip keeps going around: when local crops are destroyed by Plan Colombia's toxic chemicals and cheap corn, cotton, and grains from US corporations flood the economy, traditional agriculture dies — and the drug mafia buys up the farmland to plant more coca and opium fields. The result: production of more Colombia White bound for more users in the United States.

The overpowering of land-based, peasant, and indigenous existence by corporate developers is crucial to the effort. According to Cecilia Zarate-Laun of the Colombia Support Network in Madison, Wisconsin, "The fight against drugs became a repressive, military-focused strategy, guided by the concept of national security for the US."[151]

Exxon Mobil of Texas is the second largest corporation in Colombia, raking in $1.4 billion a year. Imperial Oil, Exxon Mobil Coal and Minerals, ESSO and Monetary Coal Company, Compañía Minera Disputa de Las Condes, International Colombia Resources

Corporation — they are *all* Exxon Mobil, and the Colombian army beat out the Wayuu natives to get the land for their endeavors.[152] DynCorp hires Eagle Aviation Services and Technology to spray herbicides on the jungles and farmlands of the Andes, and DynCorp has a long history of CIA collaboration. In 2001 the International Labor Rights Fund filed suit in US district court on behalf of 10,000 Amazonian natives and peasant farmers, charging wrongful death, torture, and infanticide for pounding them with toxic chemicals.[153] The US-Colombian Business Partnership has lobbied incessantly for increased military aid — representing Occidental Petroleum, BP Amoco, Enron, Colgate-Palmolive, Texaco, Caterpillar, Bechtel, and Philip Morris. This last player — with headquarters in New York City and factories in Kentucky, North Carolina, and Virginia — was slapped with a civil suit in 2000, alleging it colludes with narcotraffickers to smuggle cigarettes into Colombia.[154]

This business of linking US-based multinationals with expansion onto native lands, exploitation of land-based peoples, and drug production is a tedious job. But an illuminating one. What about Dole Food

Company that controls banana farming and 25 percent of the US-bound cut-flower industry?[155] Drummond Oil that mines coal while developing real estate? Coca Cola? Occidental? Evidence exists that Citibank processes the money made by drug barons so it can be pumped into further expansion of corporate projects, further demise of land-based sustainability — and further development of drug crops.[156]

It's probably fitting to mention at this point that a corporation looking to borrow money for a new project — say, an oil refinery — can do so legally at 9 percent. Or can borrow laundered drug money at ... *6 percent.*[157]

Aaaa-ah, the right hand. The US is punitive: it vehemently opposes drug education, syringe exchanges, safe injection rooms, overdose prevention; it pushes anti-drug repression as proof of fitness for participation in corporate free-trade markets; it withholds aid to countries (Nigeria) that do not enact urine testing, arrest quotas, and mass roundups.

The left. The US government closes it eyes, colludes, and/or jumps right in: it sends military technology to regimes (Colombia, Bolivia, Afghanistan) whose officials are receptive to corporate exploitation

— and that also tolerate, encourage, or invest the spoils of illicit narcotics production.[158]

A rough-hewn circle of support, made up of all the clients and staff at the treatment center, launched Joaquin's departure. We heard some good words about keeping steady, the Serenity Prayer, an inspirational song — and suddenly Joaquin was sitting shotgun in my car.

It was October. Despite all the effort made by the staff at Embudo, he was edgy. He borrowed the Jeep to run a few errands in Española and when he returned the gas gauge, which had read full at departure, was on empty. He complained that the bedroom had become an intolerable replica of a jail cell. He yanked the wires out of the Jeep's radio. And when anyone asked how he was, he answered too loudly and too mechanically with a string of "good, good, good, goods."

Something was erupting, and in the face of whatever dragon it represented, Joaquin was unhinging.

How you bring the stuff in.

From Burma. At this point, it's touchy business for the country with the world's worst human-rights record to send exports directly into the US. FedEx announces on its website that all shipments have been disbanded. UPS doesn't even list Burma. If you have heroin you want transported to the US, you might try stepping onto a Myanmar Airways flight bound for Mexico City, then take a bus to Los Angeles. You could stash the goods in a sealed shipping container stacked with hardwood, headed out on Myanmar Five Star Line to Singapore; then pitch all record of the first leg of the trip and move from there. You could place your product on an army-sponsored caravan to the Yunnan border with China. Or the border with Thailand at Ban Phai. Then swallow it in a honey-flavored condom and cozy into first class from Bangkok to JFK.

How you bring *chiva* into the United States.

Colombia. This is easier. Pack it in your suitcase and step onto your own private plane. Stow it in your carry-on bag on Avianca Air to Mexico City. Or your wheelchair. Or your computer hard drive. Stitch it into the lining of your jacket and board an Intercontinental flight to Miami. Hide it in a refrigerator container of cut flowers inside an LCL Navigation tanker headed for Florida.

From Mexico. The task is easiest yet. Stuff it into the air filter of a Dodge Ram Charger. Put it in the battery of a Nissan Sentra. Place it on the oil pan of a tractor-trailer. Cut it into the heel of your Roper boots and walk across. Pop it into a package and drop it off at the Asociación Mexicana de Transitarios. Cart it through an underground tunnel to Texas.

From Afghanistan. A little goes a long way. Pack your morphine bricks in burlap bags on a mule and trek east through the Hindu Kushi mountains to a lab at the Pakistani border; stuff the resulting heroin into a balloon in your vagina; hop on an Ariana Afghan flight to Frankfort. Roll your narcotics into tiny plastic baggies and hide them in a shipping container full of almonds, headed on a Soviet-made truck for Iran. Transfer the container onto a cargo ship bound for Southampton, England. Down a bite-size bag with coffee and fly to New York.

Afghanistan.

Burma/Southeast Asia lost its position as top heroin producer to the world in 2003, after the US toppled the opium-suppressing Taliban and ushered in a regime built of the opium-dependent Northern Alliance and a potpourri of jockeying tribal chiefs.[159]

While a reality of corporate pipelines, energy grids, shopping malls, and fear-factored TV may lie in somebody's idea of Afghanistan's future, right now Afghani society is volatile as all get-out — what with the destruction of roads, villages, and local economies; and ensuing poverty and social chaos. In the wake of this predicament, half of the economy is now based on poppy growing and heroin production,[160] and is predicted to surge by another 30 percent.[161] And so the US, at this point aiming only for a modicum of stability as it pursues its battle against terrorists elsewhere, is turning its notorious blind eye — as an example toward Haji Bashar, once commander of an opium empire that helped finance the Taliban, now switching his loyalty to the US-backed authorities.[162] Most of the nations new crop — estimated at between 75 percent[163] and 95 percent[164] of the world's total — goes to Asian, African, and European addicts.

Inside the US, heroin marketers do business on their own turf. Los Angeles-based Mexicans control everything west of the Mississippi. Nigerians in Chicago peddle dope to the Midwest. Chinese gangs sell in places like San Francisco that have large Asian communities, and Dominican syndicates fronting for Colombian cartels operate out of New York City. Now that Colombian cartels have entered the heroin market, they give their cocaine customers free samples of *chiva*, touting it as a good way to come down off a cocaine rush.

Addiction takes off where the traffickers want it to take off. Blacks in South Central LA. Middle-class kids in the suburbs of Baltimore. Chinese villagers along the drug routes from Burma and Thailand. Students in Mexico. AIDS patients in Italy. Vietnamese school kids. *Norteños.*

Joaquin started to pee on the toilet seat. In the year and a half we had lived together, he had never missed the bowl. I took his behavior as a sign.

The former chief of police was now his court-ordered confidante/parole officer, and this was a fortunate development indeed. But the way Joaquin's psyche was set up, there always had to be an oppressor-enemy. The parole officer was just too natty in his suits, too harsh in his adherence to legal standards, too disconnected from his Chicano roots, whatever: the parole officer had always played the oppressor-enemy. Now, apparently, with no such receptacle in sight, *I* was destined to play the role. But since I held no real power over Joaquin and wasn't acting maliciously, he was going to have to lure me into it. A fight pitting bathroom sanitation against freedom of action would have done the trick.

I am seasoned in the art of not playing roles in other people's psychologically-motivated scripts. Smarter and more persistent theater directors than Joaquin had gone before and, instead of finding a willing actor, had been shown the stage door. After a few low-key discussions about the immediate problem — followed by more puddles of urine and more pleas of "Oh! I didn't even notice!" — I could see his game rounding the bend toward home stretch, its destination: *my* home. I skipped right over the Clorox-tissues-by-the-bowl solution and asked Joaquin to leave.

It was a frozen night in November. I knew he didn't have a place to sleep — his own house would be an icebox and his family wasn't keen on saving him — but seeing that he had become hell-bent on tripping me up for the satisfaction of inner drama, I didn't feel safe, even for one more night. I handed him a Mexican *serape* and opened the front door.

# XI.

**D**ragon! Riding the wind. Eagle, crocodile, and lion combined.

The Dragon rises up something fierce from the wooden feet of El Señor de Esquípulas. The walls of the Santuario's altar are instantly flaming like embers in an *horno* oven, the air churning in fiery gusts. The pilgrims scream, bolt from their pews, claw over each other toward the pine doors that open onto the yard. Joaquin flails. He falls, is pinned down by ... by *what?*

It's a fallen *viga*, no a shard of timber, no it's a leg … an enormous leg … the leg of a dismembered cockroach. Flames rage over Joaquin like a blanket of orange and red and yellow, and everyone in his universe — his father Loretta a swirl of judges and parole officers Ricky Razo the priest from Holy Family Armando Vibanco Contreras the social worker his mother me — everyone dissolves into a hole in the floor like melted wax.

The police report determined that the fire had been started by a live coal that leaped from the potbelly stove onto the shag rug of the trailer. Mrs. Cruz was insistent: she had latched the iron door before she and her husband had left for church. When they returned, they walked into a scene from *Third Watch:* flames and smoke, flashing lights, men in canvas slickers, fire trucks from three villages — and Joaquin was there. He claimed he had struggled to put out the blaze with a garden hose, but that it had been as useless as a tourniquet frozen in ice.

"Don't expect anything from me," he pleads in what becomes our last conversation. "I'm just a drug addict." Joaquin. Son of Chimayó. Student of East LA. *Vato*. *Ese*. I do not make my departure from our love with remorse. An Anglo in Chimayó chides me. "You should have seen it coming," he insists from atop some high horse he has saddled up, speaking as if an incomparable disaster has overshadowed my being. He doesn't understand: for one glorious year and a half I was given an opportunity to share in the vital presence of a man unfolding into what was for him a new life, a life that celebrated the elegant beauty of the inseparability of suffering from joy. Most importantly, I never viewed Joaquin as a project; he was a partner.

Dear Joaquin.

Last seen sucking Camel filters in the shadows of the doorjam to a *tiendita* up the mountain all *suavecito* on the surface. Last glimpsed hightailing it up Route 76 in a snow storm, tripping over ragged bedroom slippers, as nervous as an abused Doberman. Last reported crumpled in a narcotic heap by a dried-up *acequia* near San Juan Pueblo.

Man/child tragically arrested by pain too piercing to remember, clumsily pressing his desperation upon a world as shattered, scattered, and harsh as broken glass.

I have two choices for making the pilgrimage. I can trek the back way by myself, over the *barrancas* and through the *arroyos* of the blessed *mal país*. Or I can walk up 76 with the crowds. This year I am carrying Linda Velarde's challenge: *we aren't praying hard enough*. This year I am praying for the village of Chimayó, for all the villages of northern New Mexico, for all the villages in a world reeling from the machinations of the global heroin trade — and from the drug itself. I am praying too for Joaquin, if not for his healing, then for his soul.

It's a big job, so I set out along 76.

Both shoulders of the two-lane road are jammed with pilgrims edging their way, footfall by footfall, the mile and a half more to the Santuario. Some of these folks have already walked fifty or 100 miles.

A child is carrying a three-foot cross festooned with a glow-in-the-dark Jesus. A man, donned in a rounded baseball cap with "DURANGO" embroidered across the front, negotiates the jagged pebbles barefoot. The KOAT-TV helicopter clips overhead. Dogs trot alongside. We come upon a table offering free cups of water. Everyone gives maneuvering space to an old man who is wielding two canes, one for each decrepit leg. Vendors are peddling roasted corn. We pass a covered booth selling acrylic blankets with La Señora de Guadalupe in reds and greens so blazing God could not have invented them. Among the bumper-to-bumper traffic, the best of Chimayó's low-rider cars make their appearance: Lolo Medina's Twelve-Stations-of-the-Cross Cadillac Seville, the iridescent purple Chevy pickup, James Coriz's two-tone hotrod.

I press each foot to the ground as if sending my plea directly to the Earth. Dear Santo Niño. Señor de Esquípulas. Do you remember Celine Martinez's cries to stop the scourge? I pray in gratitude for your help. I pray for more. Dear Guadalupe, I am praying as hard as I can. *Please.*

At Ortega's weaving shop, where 76 meets Juan Medina Road, the pilgrimage spontaneously splits into two threads. Most of the walkers stay on the main route; a trickling crosses to the road that passes behind

La Plaza del Cerro. I join them. Our footfalls echo like rabbit pads on the tar, and we are framed by the branches of bare olive trees.

We come to the apple orchard where Danny Chavez's body was found. A shrine has been fashioned here. At its center stand two home-welded crosses: one boasting a brass plaque that reads "SENSELESSLY MURDERED/DANNY CHAVEZ/BORN: 12-24-66/DIED: 9-1-98"; the other made of rebar, at its center a heart of now-faded cloth carnations. Photos of Danny as a boy hang from a strand of barbed wire, and there is a separate altar for each holiday: wooden sticks topped with happy pumpkin faces; a juniper tree festooned in silver tinsel and tattered ribbon balls; and for this holy day, a wreath made of sparkly styrofoam eggs.

The Chavez family insists their Danny was a non-user and an innocent victim of drug violence. Upon capture, the alleged killer hung himself in his jail cell.

Just beyond the orchard we re-mount Juan Medina and flow back into the stream of walkers. The sky is as blue as turquoise. At the stone wall in front of Rancho de Chimayó, a row of Mexicans is leaning against the rocks, looking heartily undocumented in their Sinaloa-style cowboy hats and hand-embroidered belts. Fifty yards up the road a group of New Mexico state policemen stands idly by enjoying the sunshine. Good Friday is treating us to a stand-off between the border-crossers and their pursuers.

The pilgrimage becomes disparate at the place where the road cuts over to the church, expressing now less the collective purpose of getting there, more the intensity of one's own mission. The Capilla de Santo Niño de Atocha radiates in the morning sun like a jewel. Lolo's wife Joan and daughter Anamaria are frenetically pouring colored syrup on snow-cones for thirsty pilgrims. Officer Lewandowski rides by on his patrol bicycle.

And there it is. The Santuario, rising out of the hill above the *potrero* like a clod of terra-cotta magic.

Indeed, Chimayó is a different place since the Penitentes' procession and the federal drug bust. "The evil-shadow, black-tar energy that gripped our lives, where I was literally afraid to go out my door, is dissipated," says Linda Pedro.[165] As Captain McShan puts it, "Burglary's always a bellwether for us,"[166] and burglarlies in the village dropped from 146 in 1999 to thirty-four in 2003.[167] We still have dealers — in Chimayó mostly out on County Road 87, and most certainly in other villages. We still have overdoses: Española Hospital treated 192 in 2002, Río Arriba sustained a total of eighteen deaths,[168] and the per-capita overdose death rate in the county is six times the national average.[169]

But the feel is less like the death grip of winter we once knew, more like the yearning of spring's first buds.

In August of 2003 Governor Bill Richardson promises $1.5 million as a one-year start-up grant toward a unified program for healing that *norteños* themselves will invent. "Unified" and "*norteños* themselves invent" are the key concepts. Lack of cohesion has characterized the effort, and echoing the sovereignty needs of land-based community, more than a few felt offended when the health department hired the outsider treatment group Amity to open the first drug treatment center.

There isn't much time. A vigorous group of county officials, treatment-center directors, policemen, teachers, ex-*tecatos*, priests, and health professionals meets at the community college in Española to fashion a plan. The conversation revolves around what is missing from Río Arriba's approach to recovery. Namely, since Amistad left the valley in a heat of controversy concerning cultural sensitivity and effectiveness, what is missing are venues for treatment and prevention geared to the specific vagaries of drug addiction in the rural north, adequate in scale to the task we face, and begot of *norteño* cultural practices.

The group grapples. The language used at these *encuentros* is a language developed within English-speaking funding and recovery agencies. Voucher treatment. Behavioral threats. Comprehensive Action Plan. Legal jurisdiction. The room is rectangular, lit by fluorescent tubes, not made of the dirt and wood that so many homes in Río Arriba are. And yet, the conversation inevitably deepens to the land. For all its straight-line codification and all the edginess over which agency or program will receive a chunk of the $1.5 million, a knowing bubbles up like the original healing spring in the *potrero* in Chimayó.

"We must factor in the land-based heritage of this valley," says Moises Gonzales of the Mexicano Land Education and Conservation Trust. "Remember that poverty breeds the kind of stress on families that can lead to substance abuse," adds Lauren Reichelt. "Look to herbs and nutrition for healing," offers Caterina Di Palma, a licensed acupuncturist who is pushing for the inclusion of the Five-Needle Technique that succeeded so spectacularly for China's addicts when Mao Tse-Tung took power. "In the face of Wal-Mart and whatever new big-box store is coming next, help our people grow their own businesses," says Amos Atencio of the community development group Siete del Norte. "Define for the governor the terms that have meaning for us: colonization, intergenerational trauma, cultural competency, community-based solutions, traditional medicine, *curanderismo*."

The upshot of the meetings is a nascent launch. The governor allots $550,000 for improvements to various buildings used for treatment.[170] The rest will go toward relatively conventional efforts: public education about drugs and their impact, crisis intervention in schools and jails, after-school youth programs, outreach to former inmates, and treatment, most of which is destined for Santa Fe county. The effort to heal in Río Arriba seems to be uphill on all fronts.

And yet, says Atencio, "This is just a beginning. We walked into a short-term approach with this money offer, and we went for it. But what we really need is the long-term — and that's up to us to create."[171]

Round about the time the FBI, DEA, state, and Río Arriba police were strapping their guns into their holsters for the 1999 drug bust, Ana Gutiérrez Sisneros and Ben Tafoya were musing about the possible use of traditional medicine in substance abuse recovery. Sisneros was a nurse, Tafoya the director at Hoy Recovery Program. They began by hosting two-hour seminars featuring local healers and herbalists. Then, in 2000, they put on what became the first of an annual fixture in the valley: a conference dedicated to a beloved *curandera* from the village of Truchas, "In Honor of Doña Sabinita Herrera: Traditional Medicine as a Culturally-Relevant Substance Abuse Treatment Intervention." Booths offering information on local herbs and samples of tinctures packed the entranceway to Northern New Mexico Community College's arts building; presentations on traditional massage, ceremony, and psychotherapy laid the groundwork for a land-based approach to recovery. The goal was to cross-pollinate the collective knowledge of local healers and to educate service providers about the possibilities for using traditional medicine in recovery. In 2004 Gutiérrez and Tafoya, with the help of organizer Teresa Juarez, put on their fifth conference in Española.

Tafoya's approach at Hoy is also rooted in tradition. The center serves 900 to 1,200 clients a year and is known for its work with alcoholics. But as Tafoya explains, "addiction is addiction" and drinkers who are also *tecatos* have been coming for years. In 2003 the program officially added drug treatment services.

Perhaps someone visiting from Boston or Vancouver might call the approach Hoy takes innovative. To Tafoya it's just "a return to the way things used to be handled in northern New Mexico. If there was a social issue, they brought in the elders. In some sense, Hoy has taken on that role."

As provisional elders, Tafoya and his dedicated team understand that the real healing power resides within each person. Reflective of the villages before the fragmentation of care proffered by US-style social services, they offer an unbroken continuum of care — from detox, medical care, and help finding housing and jobs through counseling, groups, and outpatient follow-up.

The healing process begins with respect; the moment a client walks through the door, he or she is treated as an individual of worth and intelligence — and since respect is so regularly a cast-off of substance abuse, he or she is also expected to treat others the same way. A poster of Malcolm X respectfully festoons the wall of Tafoya's office, along with photos of lively friends and colleagues at progressive political gatherings. He links *norteños'* experiences of disrespect, and their subsequent mirroring of it, with the area's history of colonization. As he puts it, a main catalyst of the urge to drugs and alcohol is the psychological devastation caused by being the chronic butt of injustice.

"When I grew up in Taos everyone was poor, maaaybe a neighbor had a television," he explains. "'Poor' in the sense that we didn't have the same material wealth the rest of the world had. In my era a lot of what we dealt with was racism. But for the kids today, they don't experience that so much. It's different. They are in a struggle with the material-wealth world and are forced into constant competition. They find themselves in stress and confusion: do I give up the values of my culture for the world of wealth? At the base of any addiction is a sense of stress and confusion — and of not feeling good about yourself."

After the drug bust, the folks at Hoy got creative. "How do we borrow from our own traditions to facilitate recovery?" Tafoya and his colleagues began to ask. They decided to structure the men's and women's groups in the same manner the Brotherhood of Penitentes is set up — as a fellowship in the spiritual sense; unlike Alcoholics Anonymous' system of hierarchical mentorship, each person supporting each other; each having "been there" both in knowing addiction and in growing up in the same environment; creating their own code of ethics for recovery and for life.

The staff at Hoy also began to look to traditional medicines of other land-based cultures. They became very interested in a non-addictive hallucinogen derived from a shrub of the west African country of Gabon. The indigenous people there use it as a stimulant while hunting and in larger doses during ceremonial rites, reporting it helps them communicate with the spirit world.

As a purified drug, the substance is called ibogaine. An addict in New Jersey named Howard Lotsof took it in 1962, expecting a psychedelic trip. Afterward he was floored to find that he no longer needed his heroin fix, at the same time he was experiencing none of the usual agonies of withdrawal. Since Lotsof's accidental discovery, researchers at the National Institute of Drug Abuse, the Food and Drug Administration, and the University of Miami have done clinical studies. Their emerging consensus is that with one or two doses, ibogaine can not only work chemically in the body to end addiction, but also help the psyche resolve past traumas that contribute to addiction. "This," says Tafoya, "is in line with our philosophy of enhancing traditional medicine."[172]

The strength of Harry Montoya's work is also tradition. *"La Cultura Cura"* is the motto of his organization Hands Across Cultures. Montoya grew up in Arroyo Seco, just south of Española. His father was from the village of Nambé, his mother from Cuartelez — and he is a *parciante* of the Acequia Rincón of Nambé. Like everyone else in these parts, Montoya has stood face-to-face with the impacts of drug addiction. "I've known a lot of what's happening since way back when I was in elementary and high school," he explains. "I've had friends and relatives who died as a result of drugs, heroin especially. The sad thing is nobody did anything proactively to keep it from happening."

If there is a second motto to the work of Hands Across Cultures, it is *"Más Vale Prevenir Que Lamentar"* / "It's Better to Prevent Problems Than to Mourn Their Effects." As Montoya describes the current situation, "You talk to kids and they tell you everything's hopeless. Now we're seeing suicidal ideation, it's almost a daily crisis at the high school. We're trying to provide hope."

The daily work of Hands Across Cultures is to offer a sense of self-worth through cultural identity and a sense of possibility through opportunity. In 1999 they published a bilingual textbook called *soy yo*, concocted by a team of high school students, on the history of northern New Mexico and its traditions. Para los Niños serves the children of Chimayó and nearby Sombrillo elementary schools with a safe after-school environment and assistance with homework. Sky'z the Limit offers classes, discussion groups, and recreational activities at the teen center. Project SUCCESS teaches students at Española Valley High School about the dangers of substance abuse. Under the guidance of Taos agricultural philosopher Miguel Santistevan, e-Plaza has developed a website to serve the agricultural communities of *el norte*; eighteen students from six school districts and various homeschooling sites conducted interviews with farmers and *acequia parciantes* to create it.

Montoya's favorite projects are the videos which explore the effects of drug and alcohol abuse, highlight northern New Mexico's history, and point to the importance of courage, honesty, and social involvement for healing. His vision is to create a Parent Corps modeled on the Peace Corps, a cadre of leaders to educate the community about the risks addictive drugs pose to children and teenagers.[173]

Meanwhile, Chimayó has seen its own vision come true. Before the drug bust, Chimayó Crime Prevention's Bruce Richardson would go to meetings with federal law enforcement officials carrying a brown paper bag. At the moment the agents began to dismiss his appeals for their involvement, as they inevitably did, Richardson would pull a five-gallon glass jar out of the bag. "I live downstream from the Barelas, and *this* is what runs in my *acequia!*" he would declare, pointing to more than a dozen capped and uncapped syringes floating in filthy grayish water. "*This* is what I irrigate my fields with." Every time a collective gasp would detonate — and then silence.

Richardson's drive to kick the drug dealers out of Chimayó expanded into a full-out process — from interdiction to rehabilitation — when he met Suellen Strale in 1997. Strale was a self-described "behavioral health freak." In her career she had coordinated programs at Jemez House Youth Center and opened a drug-treatment center in Española offering horseback riding, caving, and river rafting. Strale lived in a "pocket of drugs and burglary" in the village, the kind of neighborhood "where the *tecatos* stole your tools, broke your windows, and burned down your house." Her approach to the situation was bold. "I told the dealers I worked with juvenile probation officers and the state police, and I knew who was breaking in. 'You come on my land again and mess with my stuff and scare my little boy, then I have a really nice .357 Magnum and I'm a good shot. *Are we making ourselves clear?*'" she explains. "I was never bothered again."

Strale and Richardson joined with Florence Jaramillo, Luís and Ruth Sandoval, and other Chimayosos, and the Youth Conservation Corps was born in 2002. When you step into its office in the old apple shed, you see the kids highlighted on a wall of photographs, smiling gleefully in work gloves with shovels in their hands. "They're 98 percent from Chimayó," says Strale, "they get paid, and the projects link them back to the land."

One project the Youth Corps has accomplished is the replanting of ponderosa pines on La Merced de Nuestra Señora del Rosario, San Fernando y Santiago after a 2001 forest fire. The land grant is the one that historically serves Chimayó. Another project was to restore the *potrero* behind the Santuario to its original pastureland condition. A third has been to landscape and restore the ditch at the hospital where Río Arriba county has opened a treatment center. A fourth has been to xeriscape senior centers in the county and, in the process, refurbish the connection between teens and *ancianos*. The group has also received government funding to clean up the Barela drug compound. "Our goal," says Strale, "is to regenerate the agrarian traditions of the village."[174]

Simultaneously, young people are themselves joining the effort to preserve the *acequias* and reclaim the land grants on their own. Carlos Trujillo was a child in the village when Josefa Gallegos bought the pink stucco house on 76 to serve as her drug store. His family is made up of both community leaders and heroin addicts. He is also, through his grandfather, an heir to La Merced de Nuestra Señora del Rosario, San Fernando y Santiago, and he grew up on the Acequia del Distrito. A party at his parent's house is a festival of home-raised fire-cooked lamb, homegrown squash, and home-brewed wine.

At twenty-one, Trujillo is a barrel of energy for revitalizing Chicano culture in the wake of colonization and the influx of drugs.

His collective of fifteen students, called Verdad, broke away from an Española-sponsored organization to go it alone "without adults." "We're in a thirty-year process of change in the valley," explains Trujillo. "The hope for Chimayó is that it's still old and rustic like a piece of clay that can be molded into a beautiful pot."

Verdad organized the annual Fiesta in Española in 2001. Not only were they the first youth group to do so, but they made unprecedented changes in the program.

The most dramatic concerned the re-enactment of the conquistador who forged the first Spanish-sponsored settlement in the valley. Verdad stripped Juan de Oñate of his armor. "We wanted to say to our native neighbors and to our own leaders, 'Hey, our problems are all the same. Poverty doesn't recognize the difference between Pueblo and Chicano.'"[175]

In 2003 Verdad worked with the Camino Real Consortium and the Embudo Valley Library to put on a four-day festival of land and water at La Merced de Sebastián in Alcalde and La Merced del Embudo de Picurís. The gathering hosted activists and historians from Chihuahua, México, whose presentations on the politics of land use put the "Me" back into "Xicano." Highlights included tours of the *acequias*, performances by Aztec dancers, and a talk by University of New Mexico sociologist Felipe Gonzales acknowledging the connection between heroin addiction and loss of land in *el norte*.

An inherent sense that life was better when the *mercedes* were intact pervades the community. Estevan Arellano is an heir to La Merced del Embudo de Picurís and *mayordomo* of the Acequia Junta y Ciénega. He is also an award-winning writer whose efforts to create local literature go back to La Academia de la Nueva Raza of the 1970s. One of his ancestors, Martín Serranos, came to the northern territory from Mexico in 1548 from Zacatecas; another, Juan Cristóbal Arellano, came from Aguascalientes in 1695.

Arellano's analysis of the changes that made his community susceptible to addiction includes the arrival of more than heroin. He speaks of the imposition in the 1930s of government subsidies that encouraged villagers to stop farming, live off welfare checks and, in some cases, sell their land. He points to the first supermarket in Española in the 1950s, Fairview Foods, which further unraveled the bonds between family, land, and sustainability. Los Alamos National Laboratory, established on the mesas above the valley to build the nation's nuclear weapons, began hiring Chicanos and natives from the pueblos, and a class system resulted: villagers with full-time salaries, even if for just pushing brooms, began to look down on family members who raised sheep, hunted, and had no money. Then, says Arellano, as heroin began to help people suppress the disorientation and suffering that such changes wrought, television added the final blow: TV shows glorifying drug dealers.

The centerpieces of Arellano's ideas for recovery involve food and libraries. He puts the two together in a homegrown conception of ecoliteracy. *Querencia*, he calls it. "Our small community libraries can play a big role in prevention and be centers for recovery," he says. "I mean not only getting people to read books, but can we read the environment? Can we read the water and the land? Do we know how our food is grown? I went to one of the *arroyos* up in Cañoncito last summer. It almost made me cry. People had dumped a whole bunch of oil. That's the equivalent to injecting a needle into your vein. The *arroyos* are the veins of the land, no? The water we drink flows underneath them. Our libraries — in Embudo, El Rito, Abiquiú, Truchas — can promote knowledge of our ecology and how we make food for ourselves."[176]

The Embudo Valley Library, where Arellano's wife Elena works, bought the old general store in Dixon and has transformed it into a community center where meetings concerning organic farming, *las mercedes*, poetry, and politics take place. The library specializes in local history and ecology and has a one-of-a-kind archive on the *acequias*. The group has also restored the field behind the buildings and planted an orchard of heirloom apple trees.

Meanwhile, the work of the religious leaders who came together after Linda Pedro's procession in the Black Tar Heroin Initiative has coalesced into a force called Interfaith Leadership for Empowerment of All People. I-LEAP. Since the group's inception it has grown to include nineteen congregations of different denominations, representing 11,000 people. A total of fifteen members has traveled to Pacific Institute for Community Organizing trainings.

The priests, ministers, yogis, and Hermanos of I-LEAP feel strongly that it is the obligation of religious institutions to address not only people's spiritual needs, but their temporal needs. "We want the church to stand with us in our struggle for social justice," explains José Villa of San Juan Pueblo Parish, "and this includes all the complex issues surrounding drug abuse." They also believe in the power of the people.

The work unfolds quietly. Much of it is accomplished one-on-one. Members mentor children, deliver socially-relevant sermons, and respond to community problems. By hosting dialogs, they facilitate communities to take on the issues that affect them most. In 2004 I-LEAP partnered with Catholic Charities to rent the old John Hyson school in Chimayó. The goal: to forge a presence that links "God and peace and love and good" with social services for families, the elderly, and children; recreational programs and job training.[177] "We want [local treatment providers] to be there for the people," explains Villa, "and be there to serve."[178]

Lastly, the work of the county has come to fruition with the purchase and renovation of Piñon Hills, an abandoned hospital in the village of Velarde. "This was a multimillion-dollar project," says Lauren Reichelt, "and *nobody* thought it could be done." The center will provide detox, inpatient treatment, outpatient follow-through, public education, and community meeting space. As of 2004, the Center is offering medically managed detox. By fall of 2005, the renovations will be finished. According to Reichelt,"If I have to spend the rest of my life on this, we're opening the place."

Wrapping up Family Care Network's efforts over the last decade, she concludes: "In terms of getting people to accept treatment as part of the solution, we've been effective. I think we've had a lot to do with raising the community's consciousness because when we first started working on the playground back in '93, it was taboo to even mention drugs. We've had the commissioners come out and say there's an addiction problem. The public is talking about it. And now we can say we're doing something about it."[179]

For land-based people, to approach problems by looking to how life was before the problems existed is as natural as a mustang mare reaching for apples. Curiously, the urge lies at the foundation of any psychotherapeutic approach to recovery: manage the symptoms that express the suffering, yes — stop the dealers, administer the Narcan, try with all your heart to work with the addicts — but ultimately, excavate to the original cause of trauma.

The original cause of the distress laying the base for *norteños'* attraction to addictive substances is colonization. The conquest most easily understood is that which took place when the US government arrived in 1848, subjecting both *norteños* and natives to a panorama of losses: of land, water, sovereignty, traditional values, cultural memory, language, self-understanding, and self-esteem.

But there's more: shock and disorientation are not experiences merely lent by the past to up-and-coming generations. Conquest persists today through the machinations of global economic forces. Voracious development companies and transnational corporations buying up what water and land rights still exist. New freeways. Wal-Mart and Lowe's Home Improvement constructed where farms once thrived, coupling low wages and worker insecurity with an onslaught of consumer temptation. And the final emblem of assimilation into placelessness: satellite television.

From the perspective of why heroin as a commodity exists in the first place and how it has made its way into our lives, the story is likewise one of colonization — of generations of tribal and land-based peoples in India, Turkey, Southeast Asia, Afghanistan, the Andes, and Mexico. The substance itself emanates agony.

Healing from the effects of both the drug and its production, then, have come to be inseparable from, as Montoya puts it, "making sure that the villages don't get disintegrated."[180]

In other words, healing is one and the same as decolonization.

Thailand. From the heart of today's Golden Triangle comes a daring endeavor. It would have to be daring. Not only is the region the #2 poppy-producing area in the world, heroin abuse is now epidemic among its hill tribes.

Kru Ba Nua Chai is a former soldier with the Thai Army and a champion kickboxer. He is also the abbot of the Golden Horse Monastery, set among the limestone boulders and bamboo forests of the northern mountains. The spiritual practice Kru Ba leads is a rigorous discipline of meditation starting at 1 a.m., chanting til dawn, calesthenics, fasting, and training in Thai-style boxing. His recruits are boys — many orphans, and some as young as seven — who hail from the impoverished families of the Hmong, Akha, Lahu, and Shan tribes. These are peoples facing grim futures in a world of shrinking farmlands and depleted forests — much of which results from generations of mass drug production. Some of the boys are former opium and heroin addicts.

Their mission: for half of each month they ride their ponies through the rocky terrain of the border with Burma. They come galloping into the villages, saffron robes flapping, to spread Buddha's teachings of compassion and traditional lifeways. Their means: to show, by their own joy, that life after heroin addiction can be meaningful and good.[181]

China. Most of the heroin used in China comes from Burma, whose traffickers are zeroing in on a market of 1.3 billion potential addicts by targeting villagers in remote border regions. *Xidu*/Inhaling Poison. From overdoses to the resulting decline in farming, the people of Ergu in Sichuan province have had enough of drug-induced tragedy. A village of 2,700, they christened their effort to rid themselves of addiction in 2003 with a toast of fresh chicken blood. Then they began nightly patrols combing Ergu and neighboring villages to hunt down users. When they find them, they talk with family members to persuade them to quit. If that doesn't work, they lock them in their homes until they are clean.[182]

Colombia. Neoliberal policies facilitating corporate exploitation of land and water, Plan Colombia's drug war, terrorism against the population by all sides of the civil conflict, the perpetration of the drug industry by all sides — the enmeshment of these forces is starkly evident. In their wake, civility has become so wasted that *any* call for peace is a protest against them all.

With unfathomable courage villages everywhere are rising up — "rebels without weapons," they are called. A local activist blew the traditional wooden instrument to round up the citizens of Puracé to stand against leftist guerrillas attempting a village takeover. Led by their pastor, the citizens of Coconuco flooded the streets waving white sheets. In the midst of an attack, Belén de los Andaquíes' residents formed a cordon made of Colombian flags and sang the national anthem. Members of the Paeces native tribe of Caldono stopped an assault by carrying torches and blaring the music of beloved human-rights singer Mercedes Sosa. In the town of Bolivia, all 28,000 residents surrounded attackers and let the air out of their tires.[183]

Defending against paramilitary and rebel blockades attempting to starve people so that they will give over their lands for drug farms, many towns have established "economies of resistance" to build food self-sufficiency and local trade between villages.

"All the armed groups present in our territories are violating the rights of the ... population," says Julio Córdoba of the department of Chocó. "We've made the decision not to be silent in the face of incursions, threats, or the killings committed by the guerrillas, the 'paras,' or the armed forces themselves."[184]

Bolivia. 2003 saw an uprising of hundreds of thousands of indigenous farmers and workers in the township of El Alto where 750,000 Aymara Indians live, having been displaced from their traditional lands by corporate gas, mining and forestry projects and by illicit drug growing. Armed with slingshots and sticks, El Alto's residents built barricades, pushed a train off its railing, clashed with police at a local Coca-Cola plant, and battled the army. "We're not going to allow ourselves to be pushed around any-more," said Bernaldo Castillo Mollo, a bricklayer who was shot in the foot during the protests. "So that our children have a better future than us, we are willing to die."[185]

One objection is the Bolivian government's com-plicity with Plan Colombia's poisoning of coca and poppy farms — and along with them every crop, per-son, and animal in the wind. Not only is coca valued as a traditional medicine in the villages of the Bolivian highlands, but the US's promise to plant alternative crops like pineapple or yucca has come to nothing, leaving the farmers worse off than before fumigation.

In the wake of the revolt, the US-friendly president flees the country. "There has to be a change that is truly Bolivian," says coca grower Dionisio Núñez, "not one that is imposed by foreigners with the pretext that eradication will put an end to narcotics trafficking."[186] For many native peoples in Bolivia, who make up 60 to 80 percent of the population, the goal is the eradication of the DEA and the re-institution of a sustainable neo-Incan Andes.

Mexico. The Zapatista movement originally arose in Chiapas in 1994 to become the most popular expression of anti-corporate globalization in the world. Its objective is indigenous cultural and land rights. In 2003 the Zapatistas reached out to native communities throughout the southern states. In opposition to Mexico's reliance on corporate food imports, they are returning to communal village farming. In rejection of Mexico's legal system, they are settling disputes by centuries-old means of village assemblies and "good government" councils — and declaring regional autonomy outside the control of national government. Banners draped across the roads announce that no drugs or alcohol are allowed, violators are expelled.

Mexico. Long ago the ancients of the Tarahumara people in Chihuahua said: "Never let them take the forest because the forest calls the rain. If they take the forest, even the people will be no more." Indeed, commercial loggers have been taking the 200-year-old pine trees in the Sierra Madre Occidental and then, when there is no more forest left, have turned the land over to the cartels. Wracked by poverty from the loss of their traditional forests, the Tarahumara are then called into service as wage-slaves to the poppy and marijuana farms that result.

In 2003 five Tarahumara women stood in the path of the logging trucks and, with only their bodies and their fierceness, proclaimed *"¡Ya Basta!"*

"What could make a person strong is understanding completely where you come from," says former Río Arriba county commission president Alfredo Montoya. He is heir to both La Merced de Sebastián Martín on his mother's side and La Merced de San Joaquin on his father's, as well as *comisionado* of the Acequia de Alcalde. "Understanding who you are. What your village has to offer. Your history. Your traditions and customs. How spiritually there's places to go. And that is why the land and water issues, fighting for the *acequias* and the land grant movement, are so important for recovering from substance abuse."[187]

I have arrived at the Santuario, and I am kneeling on the floor of the *posito*. From down here, the only things I can see are cracked hiking boots, scuffed athletic shoes — and the carved-out hole that contains the Holy Dirt. I dip my fingers into the soil, rub some into the center of my forehead, dab a few grains on my tongue.

Esquípulas. Dear Santo Niño: we are your servants. Guadalupe, please.

*Inspire us with the strength we will need.*

# ENDNOTES

1.  "Economic and Social Consequences of Drug Abuse and Illicit
    Trafficking," No. 6, United Nations Office on Drug Control and
    Crime Prevention, New York, August 2002, p. 3; and Michael
    Ruppert, *Crossing the Rubicon: The Decline of the American Empire at
    the End of the Age of Oil*, Gabriola, BC Canada, New Society
    Publishers, 2004, p. 61.
2.  "Heroin and Opium Consumption," *Heroin Movement Worldwide*,
    United States Central Intelligence Agency, McLean VA, April 5,
    2001; "The Supply of Illicit Drugs to the United States," Drug
    Enforcement Administration, National Narcotics Intelligence
    Consumers Committee Report, 1995, August 1996, pp. vii-ix;
    "The UN Giveth, and the Drug Trade Prospereth," *High Times*,
    December 15, 1999; and Michael Ruppert, *Crossing the Rubicon*,
    p. 63.
3.  Testimony of Rogelio Guevara, Chief of Operations, US Drug
    Enforcement Administration, House Government Reform
    Committee, December 12, 2002.

4. Derrick Jensen, "Tricks of the Trade: Alfred McCoy on How the CIA Got Involved in Global Drug Trafficking," *The Sun*, No. 329, May 2003.

5. "2001 National Household Survey on Drug Abuse," Public Health Service, US Department of Health and Human Services, Rockland MD, 2001.

6. "New Mexico Drug Abuse-Related Mortality Rates, 1993-1995," Bureau of Vital Records and Health Statistics, Public Health Division, New Mexico Department of Health, Santa Fe NM, 1996.

7. "United States Census 2000," Department of Commerce, Washington DC, 2001; "Problem Statement," Project Reference 398022, Río Arriba Family Care Network, Española NM, 1998, p.1; and conversation with Moises Gonzales, Río Arriba County Planning and Zoning Department, Española NM, July 12, 2002.

8. Conversation with New Mexico State Police Captain Quintin McShan, Española NM, July 15, 2002.

9. S.F. Hurley, "Effectiveness of Needle Exchange Programs for Prevention of HIV Infection," *Lancet*, No. 349, 1997, p. 1797.

10. R. Heimer, K. Khoshnood, F.B. Jariwala, B. Duncan, Y. Harima, "Hepatitis in Used Syringes," *Journal of Infectious Diseases*, No. 173, 1996, pp. 997-1000.

11. "Association Between Heroin Use, Needle Sharing, and Hepatitis B and C Positivity," New Mexico Department of Health, Santa Fe NM, 2001.

12. "The World Opium Situation," US Bureau of Narcotics and Dangerous Drugs, Washington DC, October 1970, p. 10; "International Narcotics Control Strategy Report, March 1990," No. 9749, US State Department, Bureau of International Narcotics Matters Washington DC, March 1990; and Alfred McCoy, *The Politics of Heroin*, Brooklyn NY, Lawrence Hill Books, 1991, p. 18.

13. Alfred McCoy, *The Politics of Heroin*, p. 38.

14. M. Copeland, *Beyond Cloak and Dagger*, Pinnacle Books, 1975; and Henrik Krüger, *The Great Heroin Coup: Drugs, Intelligence, and International Fascism*, Montreal, Black Rose Books, 1980, p. 34.

15. John Cusack, "Turkey Lifts the Poppy Ban," *Drug Enforcement*, Fall 1974, p. 3; and Alfred McCoy, *The Politics of Heroin*, p.48.

16. Alfred McCoy, *The Politics of Heroin*, p. 73.

17. Henrik Krüger, *The Great Heroin Coup*, p. 124.

18. CBS News Report, June 17, 1971; and Henrik Krüger, *The Great Heroin Coup*, p. 124.

19. Henrik Krüger, *The Great Heroin Coup*, p. 126.

20. Alfred McCoy, *The Politics of Heroin*, p. 162.

21. *New York Times*, September 17, 1963, p. 45; and Alfred McCoy, *The Politics of Heroin*, p. 162.

22. Robert Taylor, "Foreign and Domestic Consequences of the KMT Intervention in Burma," Data Paper No. 93, Southeast Asia Program, Cornell University, Ithaca NY, 1973; "Kuomintang Aggression against Burma," Ministry of Information, Union of Burma, Rangoon, 1953; and Alfred McCoy, *The Politics of Heroin*, pp. 162 and 169.

23. Alfred McCoy, *The Politics of Heroin*, p. 178.

24. *Hong Kong Standard*, October 17, 1970; and Alfred McCoy, *The Politics of Heroin*, p. 271.

25. Catherine Lamour and Michel Lamberti, *The International Connection: Opium from Growers to Pushers*, New York, Pantheon, 1974, p. 117; and Alfred McCoy, *The Politics of Heroin*, p. 289.

26. *New York Times*, June 6, 1971, p.2; and Alfred McCoy, *The Politics of Heroin*, pp. 222 and 288.

27. NACLA Report, October 1972; and Henrik Krüger, *The Great Heroin Coup*, p. 124.

28. "The Drug Abuse Problem in Vietnam," Report of the Office of the Provost Marshall, US Military Assistance Command Vietnam, Saigon, 1971, p. 6; and Alfred McCoy, *The Politics of Heroin*, pp. 223.

29. US Executive Office of the President, Special Action Office for Drug Abuse Prevention, "The Vietnam Drug User Returns: Final Report," Washington DC, 1974, p. 57; and Alfred McCoy, *The Politics of Heroin*, p. 258.

30. *Drug Enforcement*, Winter 1975, cited in US House Committee on International Relations, "The Narcotics Situation in Southeast Asia: The Asian Connection," 9th Congress, 1st Session, Washington DC, 1975, p. 49.

31. *New York Times*, August 11, 1971, p. 1; *New York Times*, November 12, 1971, p. 93; *Christian Science Monitor*, November 16, 1972; and Alfred McCoy, *The Politics of Heroin*, p. 259.

32. Hank Messick, *Lansky*, New York, Putnam, 1971, p. 241; and Alfred McCoy, *The Politics of Heroin*, p. 253.

33. Interview by Alfred McCoy with an agent of the US Bureau of Narcotics and Dangerous Drugs, Washington DC, November 18, 1971; *New York Times*, January 9, 1972, p. 25; and Alfred

McCoy, *The Politics of Heroin*, p. 254.

34. Alfred McCoy, *The Politics of Heroin*, p. 253.

35. US Congress, House Committee on International Relations, "The Shifting Pattern of Narcotics Trafficking: Latin America," 94th Congress, 2nd Session, Washington DC, 1976, pp. 7-13; US Drug Enforcement Administration, "Heroin Source Identification for US Heroin Market" Washington DC, Unpublished documents, 1972, 1973, 1974, 1975; and Alfred McCoy, *The Politics of Heroin*, p. 392.

36. Lester Wolff, et al., "The Narcotics Situation in Southeast Asia," *Drug Enforcement*, Summer 1975, pp. 28-33; and Alfred McCoy, *The Politics of Heroin*, p. 391.

37. US Congress, House Committee on International Relations, "The Narcotics Situation in Southeast Asia: The Asia Connection," 94th Congress, 1st Session, Washington DC, 1975, p. 40; and Alfred McCoy, *The Politics of Heroin*, p. 391.

38. US House Committee on International Relations, "The Narcotics Situation in Southeast Asia," p. 38.

39. Lester Wolff, et al., "The Narcotics Situation in Southeast Asia," pp. 28-33.

40. John Cusack, "Turkey Lifts the Poppy Ban," pp. 3-7; and Alfred McCoy, *The Politics of Heroin*, p. 392.

41. House Committee on International Relations, "The Shifting Pattern of Narcotics Trafficking: Latin America," pp. 7-13; US Drug Enforcement Administration, "Heroin Source Identification," and Alfred McCoy, *The Politics of Heroin*, p. 392.

42. "International Narcotics Control Strategy Report," March 1990, Bureau of International Narcotics Matters, p. 20; and Alfred McCoy, *The Politics of Heroin*, p. 387.

43. *New York Times*, February 11, 1990; and Alfred McCoy, *The Politics of Heroin*, p. 397.

44. "International Narcotics Control Strategy Report, March 1990", Bureau of International Narcotics Matters, p. 20; and Alfred McCoy, *The Politics of Heroin*, p. 387.

45. "Controlling Drug Abuse: A Status Report," US Comptroller General, Washington DC, March 1, 1988, pp. 11-13; and Alfred McCoy, *The Politics of Heroin*, p. 440.

46. "International Narcotics Control Strategy Report, March 1990," Bureau of Narcotics Affairs, pp. 19-20; and Alfred McCoy, *The Politics of Heroin*, p.447.

47. Lawrence Lifschulz, "Dangerous Liaison: The CIA-ISI

Connection" *Newsline*, Karachi, Pakistan, November 1989, pp. 52-53; and Alfred McCoy, *The Politics of Heroin*, p. 451.

48. Kathy Evans, "The Tribal Trail," *Newsline*, Karachi, Pakistan, December 1989, p. 26; and Alfred McCoy, *The Politics of Heroin*, p. 454.

49. "National Survey on Drug Abuse in Pakistan," Pakistan Narcotics Control Board, Islamabad, 1986, p. iii, ix, 23, 308; Zahid Hussain,"Narcopower: Pakistan's Parallel Government?" *Newsline*, Karachi, Pakistan, December 1989, p. 17; and Alfred McCoy, *The Politics of Heroin*, p. 455.

50. Maureen Orth, "Afghanistan's Deadly Habit," *Vanity Fair*, March 2002, p. 170.

51. Derrick Jensen, "Tricks of the Trade: Alfred McCoy on How the CIA Got Involved in the Global Drug Trade," Unedited online version, May 2003, p. 23, <http://www.derrickjensen.org/mccoy.html>.

52. Barry Meier, "Most Afghan Opium Grown in Rebel-Controlled Areas," *New York Times*, October 5, 2001; "Afghani Ban on Growing of Opium is Unraveling," *New York Times*, October 22, 2001, pp. B1 and B6; and Orth, "Afghanistan's Deadly Habit," p. 152.

53. Doug Lorimer, "Afghanistan: World's Largest Source of Heroin," *Green Left Weekly*, July 2, 2003.

54. Conversation with Linda Velarde, Taos NM, January 24, 2004.

55. Paul B.Weill, "The Structure of Morphine," *Bulletin on Narcotics*, Vol. II, No. 2, April 1950, p. 8.

56. Harry Magdoff, *Imperialism: From the Colonial Age to the Present*, New York, Monthly Review Press, 1978, pp. 29-35.

57. See: Robert Bly, *Iron John*, Reading MA, Addison-Wesley, 1990.

58. Thomas DeQuincey, *Confessions of an English Opium-Eater*, London, J.M. Dent, 1907, 1821.

59. J.F. Richards, "The Indian Empire and Peasant Production of Opium in the Nineteenth Century," *Modern Asian Studies*, Vol. 15, No. 1, 1981, pp. 59-62.

60. "International Opium Commission Report," Vol. 2, International Opium Commission, pp. 44-66; and *Statistical Abstracts, 1915*, US Department of Commerce, Washington DC, p. 713.

61. Sally Denton, "Dixon Heroin Ring Operates Unmolested by Law Officers," *Río Grande Sun*, January 12, 1978, p. A1.

62. A.J. Beck, *Prisoners in 1999*, US Department of Justice, Office of Justice Programs, Bureau of Justice Studies, Washington DC,

2000; and C.J. Mumola, *Substance Abuse Treatment, State and Federal Prisons, 1997*, US Department of Justice, Office of Justice Programs, Bureau of Justice Statistics, Washington DC, 1999.

63. Conversation with Captain Quintin McShan, New Mexico State Police Headquarters, Española NM, July 15, 2002.

64. Conversation with Detective Michael Quiñones, Santa Fe NM, December 15, 2003.

65. Conversation with Detective Michael Quiñones.

66. Quoted in Geoff Grammer, "Death Grip," *Santa Fe New Mexican*, June 13, 2004, page A1.

67. Tim Golden, "Afghan Ban on Growing of Opium Is Unraveling," *New York Times*, October 22, 2001, p. B6.

68. Maureen Orth, *Afghanistan's Deadly Habit*, p. 152.

69. Tim Golden, "Afghan Ban on Growing," p. B6.

70. Tim Golden, "Afghan Ban on Growing," pp. B1 and B6.

71. Maureen Orth, "Afghanistan's Deadly Habit," p. 166.

72. International Narcotics Control Strategy Report 2001, US State Department, Bureau of International Narcotics and Law Enforcement Affairs, Washington DC, 2001; and Bruce Bagley, "Drug Trafficking, Political Violence, and US Policy in Colombia in the 1990s," paper presented in Colombia In Context Conference, University of California Berkeley, February 7, 2001.

73. "Plan Colombia: A Closer Look," Information Network of the Americas, June 25, 2002, p. 1.

74. "Plan Colombia: A Closer Look," p. 2.

75. Peter Dale Scott, "The Politics of Global Drug Trafficking," Alternative Radio, PO Box 551, Boulder Co 80306, April 4, 1995.

76. Speech by Carlos Alberto Palacios, Santa Fe Community College, Santa Fe NM, April 6, 2001; and Peter Canby, "Latin America's Longest War," *The Nation*, August 16, 2004, p. 34.

77. Interview with David Corcoran on "Friday Forum with Steven Spitz," KUNM-FM Radio, Albuquerque NM, February 13, 2004; and Peter Canby, "Latin America's Longest War," p. 31.

78. Marcel Ides, "Have I Got a Plan for Colombia!" *EcoSolidaridad-Andes Libre*, May 18, 2002.

79. "Plan Colombia: A Closer Look," pp. 11-12.

80. Kirk Semple, "Afghan Effort May Shift Heroin Sales," *Boston Globe*, January 20, 2002.

81. International Narcotics Control Strategy Report 2001, US State

Department, 2001; and Kirk Semple, "Afghan Effort."

82. Kevin Hall, "Smugglers Open New Routes for Trafficking Colombian White Heroin," Knight Ridder Newspapers, November 3, 2003.

83. Testimony of Donnie Marshall, Chief of Operations, Drug Enforcement Administration, Subcommittee on National Security, International Affairs and Criminal Justice, Washington DC, July 9, 1997.

84. Ibon Villelabeitia, "Colombian Judge Orders Cali Drug Lords Freed," Reuters, November 2, 2002.

85. Michael Ruppert, *Crossing the Rubicon*, p. 78.

86. Secretaría de Relaciones Exteriores, "México y Estados Unidos ante el Problema de las Drogas, Estudio-Diagnóstico Conjunto," Ciudad de México, Formación Gráfica SA de CV, Mayo 1997, pp. 102-103; and Luís Astorga, "Drug Trafficking in Mexico: A First General Assessment," Discussion Paper No. 36, United Nations Educational, Scientific and Cultural Organization, 1999, p. 21, <http://www.unesco.org/most/astorga.htm>.

87. "Nearly 200 Arrested in Heroin Bust," *Santa Fe New Mexican*, June 16, 2000, pp. A1 and A6.

88. Quoted in Daniel Chacón, "They're Still Addicted," *Santa Fe New Mexican*, December 19, 1999.

89. Conversation with Captain Quintin McShan.

90. Brendan Smith, "Drug Deaths Continue After Raids," *Albuquerque Journal*, October 4, 1999.

91. Quoted in Brendan Smith, "Drug Deaths Continue After Raids."

92. "National Drug Control Strategy Report, February 2002," Office of National Drug Control Policy, Washington DC, February 2002, pp. 29-31; and Ann Harrison, "Counting the Costs of the Drug War," May 7, 2004, <www.alternet.org/drugreporter/18641/>.

93. Gary Johnson, "Another Prohibition, Another Failure," *New York Times*, December 30, 2000; and Judy Mann, "Support Grows for Sensible Drug Policies," *Washington Post*, January 10, 2001.

94. Michael Ruppert, *Crossing the Rubicon*, p. 18.

95. Gary Johnson, "Another Prohibition, Another Failure."

96. "Federal Bureau of Prisons Quick Facts," US Federal Bureau of Prisons, May 2002, < www.bop.gov/fact0598.html>.

97. "By the Numbers," *Albuquerque Journal*, August 19, 2002.

98. "Analysis and Synthesis," Arrestee Drug Abuse Monitoring, US Department of Justice, National Institute of Justice,

Washington, DC, 2000.

99. "Final Report of Treatment at Amistad, Española, New Mexico," Amity, Inc., Tucson AZ, 2002.

100. "Río Arriba Community Health and Justice Technical Assistance Response Team Report," US Department of Justice, Office of Justice Programs, Washington DC, August 1999.

101. Gary Johnson, "Another Prohibition, Another Failure."

102. Silja Ja Talvi, "The Color of the War on Drugs," *Santa Fe Reporter*, October 9-15, 2002, p.14; and "Race and the Drug War," Drug Policy Alliance, <http://drugpolicy.org/race/>.

103. "Río Arriba Comprehensive Community Health Profile," 2003, Río Arriba Department of Health and Human Services, Española NM, 2003.

104. "Río Arriba Comprehensive Community Health Profile," 2003.

105. "Río Arriba Comprehensive Community Health Profile," 2003.

106. Conversation with Felicia Trujillo, Nambé NM, December 12, 2003.

107. Bernardo Attias, "Towards a Rhetorical Geneaology of the War on Drugs," <www.csun.edu/~hfspc002/xxx.html>.

108. "New Mexico Governor Calls for Legalizing Drugs," News Report CNN, October 6, 1999.

109. *Santa Fe New Mexican*, October 2, 1999.

110. Mark Hummels, "Councilor to Present Anti-Drug Resolution," *Santa Fe New Mexican*, October 8, 1999, p. A1.

111. Quoted in David Collins, "Drug Abuse Continues Unabated Despite State Efforts," *Río Grande Sun*, March 6, 2003, p. A4.

112. David Collins, "Drug Abuse Continues Unabated," p. A4.

113. Conversation with a member of La Fraternidad Piadosa de Nuestro Padre Jesús Nazareno, Chimayó NM, November 18, 2003.

114. Gustavo Gutiérrez, *A Theology of Liberation*, Sister Caridad Inda and John Eagleson (eds. and trans.), Maryknoll NY, Orbis Books, p. 172.

115. Conversation with Alfredo Montoya, Española NM, February 3, 2004.

116. Conversation with Lauren Reichelt, Española NM, January 15, 2004.

117. Quoted in Barbara Ferry, "Making a Dent in Death," *Santa Fe New Mexican*, June 13, 2004, p. 3 of "Heroin: Revisiting

Río Arriba County."

118. Conversation with Lauren Reichelt.

119. Conversations with Ben Tafoya, Lauren Reichelt, and Alfredo Montoya.

120. Marshall Clinard and Richard Quinney, *Criminal Behavior Systems*, New York, Holt, Rinehart and Winston, 1967, p. 178.

121. Robert Merton, "Social Problems and Sociological Theory" in Robert Merton and Robert Nisbit (eds.), *Contemporary Social Problems*, New York, Harcourt, Brace and World, 1966, pp. 808-811.

122. Conversation with Lorenzo Valdez, Española NM, December 11, 1996.

123. See: Ward Churchill and Jim Vander Wall, *Agents of Repression: The FBI's Secret Wars Against the Black Panther Party and the American Indian Movement*, Boston, South End Press, 1988, 2002; and Ward Churchill and Jim Vander Wall, *The COINTELPRO Papers: Documents from the FBI's Secret Wars Against Dissent in the United States*, Boston, South End Press, 1990, 2002.

124. See: Gary Webb, *Dark Alliance: The CIA, the Contras, and the Crack Cocaine Explosion*, New York, Seven Stories Press, 1998, 1999.

125. Peter Dale Scott, "Drug Trafficking, Drug Wars, and the CIA," Alternative Radio, PO Box 551, Boulder CO 80306, June 10, 2000.

126. Conversation with Antionette Tellez-Humble, Santa Fe NM, January 16, 2004.

127. John Reed, "Villa Asesino, Bandido y Consumado Hombre Malo," *The World*, May 8, 1914; and Ramón Puente, "La Verdadera Historia de Pancho Villa, Por Su Médico y Secretario," *Excélsior*, March 23, 1931.

128. Ramón Puente, "Francisco Villa," *Historia de la Revolución Mexicana*, México, 1936, pp. 240-241; and Enrique Krauze, *Mexico: A Biography of Power*, New York, Harper Perennial, 1997, p. 306.

129. John Reed, *Insurgent Mexico*, Reprint, Berlin, 1936, p. 123; and Enrique Krauze, *Mexico*, p. 308.

130. Roberto Blanco Moheno, *Pancho Villa Que Es Su Padre*, México, 1969, pp. 175-178; and Enrique Krauze, *Mexico*, p. 306.

131. Enrique Krauze, *Mexico*, p. 278.

132. Enrique Krauze, *Mexico*, p. 295.

133. Enrique Krauze, *Mexico*, p. 295.

134. S. Mednik, J. Volavka, W. Gabrielli, and T. Itil, "EEG as a Predictor of Antisocial Behavior," *Criminology*, Vol. 19, 1981, pp. 219-231.

135. B.E. Wexler, "Cerebral Laterality and Psychiatry: A Review of the Literature," *American Journal of Psychiatry*, Vol. 137, No. 3, 1980, pp. 279-291; and L. Yeudall, D. Fromm-Auch, and P. Davies, "Neuropsychological Impairment of Persistent Delinquincy," *Journal of Nervous and Mental Disorders*, Vol. 170, 1982, pp. 257-265.

136. J.M. Charcot, "Leçons sur les Maladies du Système Nerveux Faites à la Salpêtrière" in A. Delahaye and E. Lecrosnie, *Progrès Medical*, Paris, 1887; and P. Janet, "Historie d'une Idèe Fixe," *Revue Philosophique*, Vol. 37, 1894, pp. 121-163.

137. See: Alfred McCoy, *The Politics of Heroin*; Peter Dale Scott, *Drugs, Oil, and War: The United States in Afghanistan, Colombia, and Indochina*, Lankam MD, Rowman and Littlefield, 2003; and Michael Ruppert, *Crossing the Rubicon*.

138. "International Narcotics Control Strategy Report, March 1997," Bureau for International Narcotics and Law Enforcement Affairs, US Department of State, Washington DC, March 1998.

139. Dennis Bernstein and Leslie Kean, "People of the Opiate:Burma's Dictatorship of Drugs," *The Nation*, December 16, 1996, p. 12.

140. "Country Commercial Guide:Burma," American Embassy, Rangoon, Burma, July 1996; and Dennis Bernstein and Leslie Kean, "People of the Opiate," p. 12.

141. Leslie Kean and Dennis Bernstein, "The Burma-Singapore Axis: Globalizing the Heroin Trade," *Covert Action*, No. 64, Spring 1998, p. 48.

142. Leslie Kean and Dennis Bernstein, "The Burma-Singapore Axis," p. 48.

143. Robert Karniol, "Myanmar Spy Centre Can Listen to Satphones," *Jane's Defence Weekly*, September 17, 1997.

144. Leslie Kean and Dennis Bernstein, "The Burma-Singapore Axis," p. 49.

145. "International Narcotics Control Strategy Report, March 1997," US State Department, p. 1.

146. "Myanmar-Singapore Ministerial-Level Work Committee Helps Develop Myanmar's Ecoonomic and Technical Sectors," *The New Light of Myanmar*, December 24, 1997.

147. "Country Commercial Guide: Burma," American Embassy, Rangoon, July 1996; and Dennis Bernstein and Leslie Kean,

"People of the Opiate."

148. Andrew Jelth, "Burma's Defense Expenditure and Arms Industries," Working Paper No. 309, Strategic and Defense Studies Center, August 1997, p. 8.

149. "Singapore: Commercial Overview," United States Commercial Service, <www.BuyUSA.gov>.

150. Juan Forero and Tim Weiner, "Colombia: Colombia, Mexico Pass Asia in Supply of Heroin to US," *Lexington Herald-Leader*, June 8, 2003.

151. Cecilia Zarate-Laun, "Introduction to Putumayo: The US-Assisted War in Colombia," Colombia Support Network, Madison WI, 2001, p. 8.

152. Jason Marti, "Eco-Terror in Colombia," July 16, 2002, p. 2, <www.andeslibre.zzn.com>.

153. Jason Marti, "Eco-Terror," p. 3.

154. Henry Weinstein, "Philip Morris Accused in Smuggling Scheme," *Latin America Times*, May 25, 2000, <www.latimes.com>.

155. Jason Marti, "Eco-Terror," p. 4.

156. Jason Marti, "Eco-Terror," p. 6.

157. Michael Ruppert, *Crossing the Rubicon*, p. 63.

158 Daniel Wolfe, "Condemned to Death," *The Nation*, April 26, 2004, pp. 14-22.

159. Doug Lorimer, "Afghanistan: World's Largest Source of Heroin," *Green Left Weekly*, July 2, 2003, p. 14; and Jerry Seper, "Afghanistan Leads Again in Heroin Production," *Washington Times*, August 2003.

160. "Morning Edition," National Public Radio, October 29, 2003; and Amy Waldman, "Afghan Route to Prosperity: Grow Poppies," *New York Times*, April 10, 2004.

161. Amy Waldman, "Afghan Route to Prosperity."

162. Mark Corcoran, "Afghanistan: America's Blind Eye" on Foreign Correspondent Radio, October 4, 2002, <http://www.abc.net.au/foreign/stories/s522030.htm>.

163. Mark Corcoran, "Afghanistan," and *Global Illicit Drug Trends 2003*, Executive Summary, United Nations Office on Drugs and Crime, New York, 2003, p. 7.

164. Doug Lorimer, "Afghanistan," p. 14.

165. Conversation with Linda Pedro, Chimayó NM, November 14, 2003.

166. Quoted in Andy Lenderman, "Northern NM Drug Crimes Dip,"

*Albuquerque Journal,* August 7, 2003.

167. Geoff Grammer, "Death Grip," p. A1.
168. Brendan Smith, "Tapping the Vein," *Santa Fe Reporter,* September 10-16, 2003, p. 18.
169. Geoff Grammer, "Death Grip," p. A1.
170. "Governor Richardson Will Put $1.5 Million Toward Río Arriba Substance Abuse Initiatives," Press release, New Mexico Department of Health, Santa Fe NM, January 7, 2004.
171. All quotes from NM Department of Health Comprehensive Regional Substance Abuse Strategy meetings, Española NM, November 2003.
172. Conversation with Ben Tafoya, Española NM, December 30, 2003.
173. Conversation with Harry Montoya, Arroyo Seco NM, December 30, 2003.
174. Conversation with Suellen Strale, Chimayó NM, November 13, 2003.
175. Conversation with Carlos Trujillo, Las Cruces NM, November 13, 2003.
176. Conversation with Estevan Arellano, Embudo NM, December 4, 2003.
177. Conversation with José Villa, La Villita NM, February 2, 2004.
178. Quoted in Colin Finan, "Interfaith Group Moves to Fill Void," *Rio Grande Sun,* June 3, 2004, pp. A1 and A3.
179. Conversation with Lauren Reichelt.
180. Conversation with Alfredo Montoya.
181. Denis Gray, "Wrath of the Little Buddhas," *Santa Fe New Mexican,* April 14, 2002, pp. F1 and F3.
182. "Inhaling Poison: Chinese Villagers Unite to Fight Heroin Scourge," *Los Angeles Times,* January 24, 2003.
183. "Rebels without Weapons: Civil Resistance against Colombia's Guerrillas," *World Press Review,* Vol. 49, No. 3, March 2002.
184. John Ludwick, "Communities in Resistance," *Latin America Press,* December 9, 2003, <www.lapress.org>.
185. "Indigenous People Flex Political Muscle," *Los Angeles Times,* October 21, 2003.
186. Larry Rohter, "Bolivian Leader's Ouster Seen as Warning on US Drug Policy," *New York Times,* October 23, 2003.
187. Conversation with Alfredo Montoya.

# ACKNOWLEDGMENTS

I extend thanks to each person from the community I have had the opportunity to work with: you are inspirational.

A number of people involved in the effort have touched me deeply. They include: Linda Pedro, the Honorable Michael Vigil, Detective Michael Quiñones, Alfredo Montoya, Ben Tafoya, Lauren Reichelt, Father Julio Gonzales, Estevan and Elena Arellano, Joseph Vigil, and Modesta and Alfonso Ruíz.

For specific help with the book, I wish to thank Hilario Romero, Lorenzo Sotelo, Antionette Tellez-Humble, Azul La Luz, Shirley and Sam Salazar, Bread for the Journey, George Morse, the Salmon and Bear Society, Estevan Arellano, Lauren Reichelt, Jesús Sepúlveda, Elisabeth Sherif, Manuel Trujillo, and John Raatz. I am indebted to Peter van Lent for ploughing through an early draft with his blue pencil, Lynn Montgomery for the modern writing tools, and my editor at New Society, Ingrid Witvoet, for her acuity and humor.

Moises Gonzales of the Mexican Land Education and Conservation Trust took time from his demanding schedule to document the to-date (2004) most accurate rendition of the *mercedes* of northern New Mexico, and his work became the template for the map of the land grants. Bill Sandoval of Buffalo Graphics came as an angel from Nambé to sift through complex geographic information and illustrate all five maps.

Finally, I am more than honored to count Judith and Chris Plant as colleagues and friends.

# INDEX